D1430127

Medium/Heavy Truck Test

Heating, Ventilation, and Air Conditioning (HVAC) Systems (Test T7)

Technical Advisor
John F. Kershaw

Africa • Australia • Canada • Denmark • Japan • Mexico • New Zealand • Philippines
Puerto Rico • Singapore • Spain • United Kingdom • United States

NOTICE TO THE READER

Publisher does not warrant or guarantee any of the products described herein or perform any independent analysis in connection with any of the product information contained herein. Publisher does not assume, and expressly disclaims, any obligation to obtain and include information other than that provided to it by the manufacturer.

The reader is expressly warned to consider and adopt all safety precautions that might be indicated by the activities herein and to avoid all potential hazards. By following the instructions contained herein, the reader willingly assumes all risks in connection with such instructions.

The Publisher makes no representation or warranties of any kind, including but not limited to, the warranties of fitness for particular purpose or merchantability, nor are any such representations implied with respect to the material set forth herein, and the publisher takes no responsibility with respect to such material. The publisher shall not be liable for any special, consequential, or exemplary damages resulting, in whole or part, from the readers' use of, or reliance upon, this material.

Delmar Staff:
Business Unit Director: Alar Elken
Product Development Manager: Jack Erjavec
Executive Marketing Manager: Maura Theriault
Channel Manager: Mona Caron
Executive Production Manager: Mary Ellen Black
Fast Cycle Production Editor: Betsy Hough
Cover Design: Paul Roseneck
Cover Image: © 1998 Corbis Corp.

Contents

Section 3 Are You Sure You're Ready for Test T7?

Section 4 An Overview of the System

Section 5 Sample Test for Practice

Section 6 Additional Test Questions for Practice

Section 7 Appendices

Preface

This book is just one of a comprehensive series designed to prepare technicians to take and pass every ASE test. Delmar's series covers all of the Automotive tests A1 through A8 as well as Advanced Engine Performance L1 and Parts Specialist P2; the series covers the five Collision Repair tests and the eight Medium/Heavy Duty truck tests.

Each book in this series has the same features designed for the technician to use and succeed with. Before a word was written, we met with and surveyed technicians and shop owners who have taken ASE tests and have used other preparatory materials. We found that they wanted, first and foremost, *lots* of practice tests and questions. Each book in our series contains a general knowledge pretest, a sample test, and additional practice questions. You will be hard-pressed to find a test prep book with more questions for you to practice with. And, we have worked hard to ensure that these questions match the ASE style in types of questions, quantities, and level of difficulty.

Technicians also told us that they wanted to understand the ASE test and to have practical information about what they should expect. We have provided that as well, including a history of ASE and a section devoted to helping the technician "Take and Pass Every ASE Test" with case studies, test-taking strategies, and test formats.

Finally, techs wanted refresher information and reference. Each of our books includes an overview section that is referenced to the task list. The complete task lists for each test appear in each book for the user's reference. There is also a complete glossary of terms for each booklet.

So whether you're looking for a sample test and a few extra questions to practice with or a complete introduction to ASE testing and support for preparing thoroughly, this book series is an excellent answer.

We hope you benefit from this book and that you pass every ASE test you take!

Your comments, both positive and negative, are most certainly encouraged! Please contact us at:

Automotive Editor
Delmar Publishers
3 Columbia Circle
Box 15015
Albany, NY 12212-5015

The History of ASE

History

Originally known as The National Institute for Automotive Service Excellence (NIASE), today's ASE was founded in 1972 as a nonprofit, independent entity dedicated to improving the quality of automotive service and repair through the voluntary testing and certification of automotive technicians. Until that time, consumers had no way of distinguishing between competent and incompetent automotive technicians. In the mid-1960s and early 1970s, efforts were made by several automotive industry affiliated associations to respond to this need. Though the associations were nonprofit, many regarded certification test fees merely as a means of raising additional operating capital. Also, some associations, having a vested interest, produced test scores heavily weighted in the favor of its members.

NIASE

From these efforts a new independent, nonprofit association, the National Institute for Automotive Service Excellence (NIASE), was established much to the credit of two educators, George R. Kinsler, Director of Program Development for the Wisconsin Board of Vocational and Adult Education in Madison, WI, and Myron H. Appel, Division Chairman at Cypress College in Cypress, CA.

Early efforts were to encourage voluntary certification in four general areas:

TEST AREA	TITLES
I. Engine	Engines, Engine Tune-Up, Block Assembly, Cooling and Lube Systems, Induction, Ignition, and Exhaust
II. Transmission	Manual Transmissions, Drive Line and Rear Axles, and Automatic Transmissions
III. Brakes and Suspension	Brakes, Steering, Suspension, and Wheels
IV. Electrical/Air Conditioning	Body/Chassis, Electrical Systems, Heating, and Air Conditioning

In early NIASE tests, Mechanic A, Mechanic B type questions were used. Over the years the trend has not changed, but in mid-1984 the term was changed to Technician A, Technician B to better emphasize sophistication of the skills needed to perform successfully in the modern motor vehicle industry. In certain tests the term used is Estimator A/B, Painter A/B, or Parts Specialist A/B. At about that same time, the logo was changed from "The Gear" to "The Blue Seal," and the organization adopted the acronym ASE for Automotive Service Excellence.

Since those early beginnings, several other related trades have been added. ASE now administers a comprehensive series of certification exams for automotive and light truck repair technicians, medium and heavy truck repair technicians, alternate fuels technicians, engine machinists, collision repair technicians, school bus repair technicians, and parts specialists.

The Series and Individual Tests

- Automotive and Light Truck Technician; consisting of: Engine Repair—Automatic Transmission/Transaxle—Manual Drive Train and Axles—Suspension and Steering—Brakes—Electrical/Electronic Systems—Heating and Air Conditioning—Engine Performance
- Medium and Heavy Truck Technician; consisting of: Gasoline Engines—Diesel Engines—Drive Train—Brakes—Suspension and Steering—Electrical/Electronic Systems—HVAC—Preventive Maintenance Inspection
- Alternate Fuels Technician; consisting of: Compressed Natural Gas Light Vehicles
- Advanced Series; consisting of: Automobile Advanced Engine Performance and Advanced Diesel Engine Electronic Diesel Engine Specialty
- Collision Repair Technician; consisting of: Painting and Refinishing—Non-Structural Analysis and Damage Repair—Structural Analysis and Damage Repair—Mechanical and Electrical Components—Damage Analysis and Estimating
- Engine Machinist Technician; consisting of: Cylinder Head Specialist—Cylinder Block Specialist—Assembly Specialist
- School Bus Repair Technician; consisting of: Body Systems and Special Equipment—Drive Train—Brakes—Suspension and Steering—Electrical/Electronic Systems—Heating and Air Conditioning
- Parts Specialist; consisting of: Automobile Parts Specialist—Medium/Heavy Truck Parts Specialist

A Brief Chronology

1970–1971   Original questions were prepared by a group of forty auto mechanics teachers from public secondary schools, technical institutes, community colleges, and private vocational schools. These questions were then professionally edited by testing specialists at Educational Testing Service (ETS) at Princeton, New Jersey, and thoroughly reviewed by training specialists associated with domestic and import automotive companies.

1971   July: About eight hundred mechanics tried out the original test questions at experimental test administrations.

1972   November and December: Initial NIASE tests administered at 163 test centers. The original automotive test series consisted of four tests containing eighty questions each. Three hours were allotted for each test. Those who passed all four tests were designated Certified General Auto Mechanic (GAM).

1973   April and May: Test 4 was increased to 120 questions. Time was extended to four hours for this test. There were now 182 test centers. Shoulder patch insignias were made available.

	November: Automotive series expanded to five tests. Heavy-Duty Truck series of six tests introduced.
1974	November: Automatic Transmission (Light Repair) test modified. Name changed to Automatic Transmission.
1975	May: Collision Repair series of two tests is introduced.
1978	May: Automotive recertification testing is introduced.
1979	May: Heavy-Duty Truck recertification testing is introduced.
1980	May: Collision Repair recertification testing is introduced.
1982	May: Test administration providers switched from Educational Testing Service (ETS) to American College Testing (ACT). Name of Automobile Engine Tune-Up test changed to Engine Performance test.
1984	May: New logo was introduced. ASE's "The Blue Seal" replaced NIASE's "The Gear." All reference to Mechanic A, Mechanic B was changed to Technician A, Technician B.
1990	November: The first of the Engine Machinist test series was introduced.
1991	May: The second test of the Engine Machinist test series was introduced. November: The third and final Engine Machinist test was introduced.
1992	May: Name of Heavy-Duty Truck Test series changed to Medium/Heavy Truck test series.
1993	May: Automotive Parts Specialist test introduced. Collision Repair expanded to six tests. Light Vehicle Compressed Natural Gas test introduced. Limited testing begins in English-speaking provinces of Canada.
1994	May: Advanced Engine Performance Specialist test introduced.
1996	May: First three tests for School Bus Technician test series introduced. November: A Collision Repair test is added.
1997	May: A Medium/Heavy Truck test is added.
1998	May: A diesel advanced engine test is introduced: Electronic Diesel Engine Diagnosis Specialist. A test is added to the School Bus test series.

By the Numbers

Following are the approximate number of ASE technicians currently certified by category. The numbers may vary from time to time but are reasonably accurate for any given period. More accurate data may be obtained from ASE, which provides updates twice each year, in May and November after the Spring and Fall test series.

There are more than 338,000 Automotive Technicians with over 87,000 at Master Technician (MA) status. There are 47,000 Truck Technicians with over 19,000 at Master Technician (MT) status. There are 46,000 Collision Repair/Refinish Technicians with 7,300 at Master Technician (MB) status. There are 1,200 Estimators. There are 6,700 Engine Machinists with over 2,800 at Master Machinist Technician (MM) status. There are also 28,500 Automobile Advanced Engine Performance Technicians and over 2,700 School Bus Technicians for a combined total of more than 403,000 Repair Technicians. To this number, add over 22,000 Automobile Parts Specialists, and over 2,000 Truck Parts Specialists for a combined total of over 24,000 parts specialists.

There are over 6,400 ASE Technicians holding both Master Automotive Technician and Master Truck Technician status, of which 350 also hold Master Body Repair status. Almost 200 of these Master Technicians also hold Master Machinist status and five Technicians are certified in all ASE specialty areas.

Almost half of ASE certified technicians work in new vehicle dealerships (45.3 percent). The next greatest number work in independent garages with 19.8 percent. Next is tire dealerships with 9 percent, service stations at 6.3 percent, fleet shops at 5.7 percent, franchised volume retailers at 5.4 percent, paint and body shops at 4.3 percent, and specialty shops at 3.9 percent.

Of over 400,000 automotive technicians on ASE's certification rosters, almost 2,000 are female. The number of female technicians is increasing at a rate of about 20 percent each year. Women's increasing interest in the automotive industry is further evidenced by the fact that, according to the National Automobile Dealers Association (NADA), they influence 80 percent of the decisions of the purchase of a new automobile and represent 50 percent of all new car purchasers. Also, it is interesting to note that 65 percent of all repair and maintenance service customers are female.

The typical ASE certified technician is 36.5 years of age, is computer literate, deciphers a half-million pages of technical manuals, spends one hundred hours per year in training, holds four ASE certificates, and spends about $27,000 for tools and equipment. Twenty-seven percent of today's skilled ASE certified technicians attended college, many having earned an Associate of Science degree in Automotive Technology.

ASE

ASE's mission is to improve the quality of vehicle repair and service in the United States through the testing and certification of automotive repair technicians. Prospective candidates register for and take one or more of ASE's thirty-three exams. The tests are grouped into specialties for automobile, medium/heavy truck, school bus, and collision repair technicians as well as engine machinists, alternate fuels technicians, and parts specialists.

Upon passing at least one exam and providing proof of two years of related work experience, the technician becomes ASE certified. A technician who passes a series of exams earns ASE Master Technician status. An automobile technician, for example, must pass eight exams for this recognition.

The tests, conducted twice a year at over seven hundred locations around the country, are administered by American College Testing (ACT). They stress real-world diagnostic and repair problems. Though a good knowledge of theory is helpful to the technician in answering many of the questions, there are no questions specifically on theory. Certification is valid for five years. To retain certification, the technician must be retested to renew his or her certificate.

The automotive consumer benefits because ASE certification is a valuable yardstick by which to measure the knowledge and skills of individual technicians, as well as their commitment to their chosen profession. It is also a tribute to the repair facility employing ASE certified technicians. ASE certified technicians are permitted to wear blue and white ASE shoulder insignia, referred to as the "Blue Seal of Excellence," and carry credentials listing their areas of expertise. Often employers display their technicians' credentials in the customer waiting area. Customers look for facilities that display ASE's Blue Seal of Excellence logo on outdoor signs, in the customer waiting area, in the telephone book (Yellow Pages), and in newspaper advertisements.

The tests stress repair knowledge and skill. All test takers are issued a score report. In order to earn ASE certification, a technician must pass one or more of the exams and present proof of two years of relevant hands-on work experience. ASE certifications are valid for five years, after which time technicians must retest in order to keep up with changing technology and to remain in the ASE program. A nominal registration and test fee is charged.

To become part of the team that wears ASE's Blue Seal of Excellence®, please contact:

National Institute for Automotive Service Excellence
13505 Dulles Technology Drive
Herndon, VA 20171-3421

2 Take and Pass Every ASE Test

ASE Testing

Participating in an Automotive Service Excellence (ASE) voluntary certification program gives you a chance to show your customers that you have the "know-how" needed to work on today's modern vehicles. The ASE certification tests allow you to compare your skills and knowledge to the automotive service industry's standards for each specialty area.

If you are the "average" automotive technician taking this test, you are in your mid-thirties and have not attended school for about fifteen years. That means you probably have not taken a test in many years. Some of you, on the other hand, have attended college or taken postsecondary education courses and may be more familiar with taking tests and with test-taking strategies. There is, however, a difference in the ASE test you are preparing to take and the educational tests you may be accustomed to.

Who Writes the Questions?

The questions on an educational test are generally written, administered, and graded by an educator who may have little or no practical hands-on experience in the test area. The questions on all ASE tests are written by service industry experts familiar with all aspects of the subject area. ASE questions are entirely job-related and designed to test the skills that you need to know on the job.

The questions originate in an ASE "item-writing" workshop where service representatives from domestic and import automobile manufacturers, parts and equipment manufacturers, and vocational educators meet in a workshop setting to share their ideas and translate them into test questions. Each test question written by these experts is reviewed by all of the members of the group. The questions deal with the practical problems of diagnosis and repair that are experienced by technicians in their day-to-day hands-on work experiences.

All of the questions are pretested and quality-checked in a nonscoring section of tests by a national sample of certifying technicians. The questions that meet ASE's high standards of accuracy and quality are then included in the scoring sections of future tests. Those questions that do not pass ASE's stringent tests are sent back to the workshop or are discarded. ASE's tests are monitored by an independent proctor and are administered and machine-scored by an independent provider, American College Testing (ACT). All ASE tests have a three-year revision cycle.

Testing

If you think about it, we are actually tested on about everything we do. As infants, we were tested to see when we could turn over and crawl, later when we could walk or talk. As adolescents, we were tested to determine how well we learned the material presented in school and in how we demonstrated our accomplishments on the athletic field. As working adults, we are tested by our supervisors on how well we have completed an assignment or project. As nonworking adults, we are tested by our family on everyday activities, such as housekeeping or preparing a meal. Testing, then, is one of those facts of life that begins in the cradle and follows us to the grave.

Testing is an important fact of life that helps us to determine how well we have learned our trade. Also, tests often help us to determine what opportunities will be available to us in the future. To become ASE certified, we are required to take a test in every subject in which we wish to be recognized.

Be Test-Wise

In spite of the widespread use of tests, most technicians are not very test-wise. An ability to take tests and score well is a skill that must be acquired. Without this knowledge, the most intelligent and prepared technician may not do well on a test.

We will discuss some of the basic procedures necessary to follow in order to become a test-wise technician. Assume, if you will, that you have done the necessary study and preparation to score well on the ASE test.

Different approaches should be used for taking different types of tests. The different basic types of tests include: essay, objective, multiple-choice, fill-in-the-blank, true-false, problem solving, and open book. All ASE tests are of the four-part multiple-choice type.

Before discussing the multiple-choice type test questions, however, there are a few basic principles that should be followed before taking any test.

Before the Test

Do not arrive late. Always arrive well before your test is scheduled to begin. Allow ample time for the unexpected, such as traffic problems, so you will arrive on time and avoid the unnecessary anxiety of being late.

Always be certain to have plenty of supplies with you. For an ASE test, three or four sharpened soft lead (#2) pencils, a pocket pencil sharpener, erasers, and a watch are all that are required.

Do not listen to pretest chatter. When you arrive early, you may hear other technicians testing each other on various topics or making their best guess as to the probable test questions. At this time, it is too late to add to your knowledge. Also the rhetoric may only confuse you. If you find it bothersome, take a walk outside the test room to relax and loosen up.

Read and listen to all instructions. It is important to read and listen to the instructions. Make certain that you know what is expected of you. Listen carefully to verbal instructions and pay particular attention to any written instructions on the test paper. Do not dive into answering questions only to find out that you have answered the wrong question by not following instructions carefully. It is difficult to make a high score on a test if you answer the wrong questions.

These basic principles have been violated in most every test ever given. Try to remember them. They are essential for success.

Objective Tests

A test is called an objective test if the same standards and conditions apply to everyone taking the test and there is only one correct answer to each question. Objective tests primarily measure your ability to recall information. A well-designed objective test can also test your ability to understand, analyze, interpret, and apply your knowledge. Objective tests include true-false, multiple-choice, fill-in-the-blank, and matching questions.

Objective questions, not generally encountered in a classroom setting, are frequently used in standardized examinations. Objective tests are easy to grade and also reduce the amount of paperwork necessary to administer. The objective tests are used in entry-level programs or when very large numbers are being tested. ASE's tests consist exclusively of four-part multiple-choice objective questions in all of their tests.

Taking an Objective Test

The principles of taking an objective test are somewhat different from those used in other types of tests. You should first quickly look over the test to determine the number of questions, but do not try to read through all of the questions. In an ASE test, there are usually between forty and eighty questions, depending on the subject matter. Read through each question before marking your answer. Answer the questions in the order they appear on the test. Leave the questions blank that you are not sure of and move on to the next question. You can return to those unanswered questions after you have finished the others. They may be easier to answer at a later time after your mind has had additional time to consider them on a subconscious level. In addition, you might find information in other questions that will help you to answer some of them.

Do not be obsessed by the apparent pattern of responses. For example, do not be influenced by a pattern like **d, c, b, a, d, c, b, a** on an ASE test.

There is also a lot of folk wisdom about taking objective tests. For example, there are those who would advise you to avoid response options that use certain words such as *all, none, always, never, must,* and *only,* to name a few. This, they claim, is because nothing in life is exclusive. They would advise you to choose response options that use words that allow for some exception, such as *sometimes, frequently, rarely, often, usually, seldom,* and *normally.* They would also advise you to avoid the first and last option (A and D) because test writers, they feel, are more comfortable if they put the correct answer in the middle (B and C) of the choices. Another recommendation often offered is to select the option that is either shorter or longer than the other three choices because it is more likely to be correct. Some would advise you to never change an answer since your first intuition is usually correct.

Although there may be a grain of truth in this folk wisdom, ASE test writers try to avoid them and so should you. There are just as many **A** answers as there are **B** answers, just as many **D** answers as **C** answers. As a matter of fact, ASE tries to balance the answers at about 25 percent per choice **A, B, C,** and **D.** There is no intention to use "tricky" words, such as outlined above. Put no credence in the opposing words "sometimes" and "never," for example. When used in an ASE type question, one or both may be correct; one or both may be incorrect.

There are some special principles to observe on multiple-choice tests. These tests are sometimes challenging because there are often several choices that may seem possible, and it may be difficult to decide on the correct choice. The best strategy, in this case, is to first determine the correct answer before looking at the options. If you see the answer you decided on, you should still examine the options to make sure that none seem more correct than yours. If you do not know or are not sure of the answer, read each option very carefully and try to eliminate those options that you know to be wrong. That way, you can often arrive at the correct choice through a process of elimination.

If you have gone through all of the test and you still do not know the answer to some of the questions, then guess. Yes, guess. You then have at least a 25 percent chance of being correct. If you leave the question blank, you have no chance. In ASE tests, there is no penalty for being wrong. As the late President Franklin D. Roosevelt once advised a group of students, "It is common sense to take a method and try it. If it fails, admit it frankly and try another. But above all, try something."

During the Test

Mark your bubble sheet clearly and accurately. One of the biggest problems an adult faces in test-taking, it seems, is in placing an answer in the correct spot on a bubble sheet. Make certain that you mark your answer for, say, question 21, in the space on the bubble sheet designated for the answer for question 21. A correct response in the wrong bubble will probably be wrong. Remember, the answer sheet is machine scored and can only "read" what you have bubbled in. Also, do not bubble in two answers for the same question. For example, if you feel the answer to a particular question is **A** but think it may be **C,** do not bubble in both choices. Even if either **A** or **C** is correct, a double answer will score as an incorrect answer. It's better to take a chance with your best guess.

Review Your Answers

If you finish answering all of the questions on a test ahead of time, go back and review the answers of those questions that you were not sure of. You can often catch careless errors by using the remaining time to review your answers.

Don't Be Distracted

At practically every test, some technicians will invariably finish ahead of time and turn their papers in long before the final call. Do not let them distract or intimidate you. Either they knew too little and could not finish the test, or they were very self-confident and thought they knew it all. Perhaps they were trying to impress the proctor or other technicians about how much they know. Often you may hear them later talking about the information they knew all the while but forgot to respond on their answer sheet.

Use Your Time Wisely

It is not wise to use less than the total amount of time that you are allotted for a test. If there are any doubts, take the time for review. Any product can usually be made better with some additional effort. A test is no exception. It is not necessary to turn in your test paper until you are told to do so.

Don't Cheat

Some technicians may try to use a "crib sheet" during a test. Others may attempt to read answers from another technician's paper. If you do that, you are unquestionably assuming that someone else has a correct answer. You probably know as much, maybe more, than anyone else in the test room. Trust yourself. If you're still not convinced, think of the consequences of being caught. Cheating is foolish. If you are caught, you have failed the test.

Be Confident

The first and foremost principle in taking a test is that you need to know what you are doing, to be test-wise. It will now be presumed that you are a test-wise technician and are now ready for some of the more obscure aspects of test-taking.

An ASE-style test requires that you use the information and knowledge at your command to solve a problem. This generally requires a combination of information similar to the way you approach problems in the real world. Most problems, it seems, typically do not fall into neat textbook cases. New problems are often difficult to handle, whether they are encountered inside or outside the test room.

An ASE test also requires that you apply methods taught in class as well as those learned on the job to solve problems. These methods are akin to a well-equipped tool box in the hands of a skilled technician. You have to know what tools to use in a particular situation, and you must also know how to use them. In an ASE test, you will need to be able to demonstrate that you are familiar with and know how to use the tools.

You should begin a test with a completely open mind. At times, however, you may have to move out of your normal way of thinking and be creative to arrive at a correct answer. If you have diligently studied for at least one week prior to the test, you have bombarded your mind with a wide assortment of information. Your mind will be working with this information on a subconscious level, exploring the interrelationships among various facts, principles, and ideas. This prior preparation should put you in a creative mood for the test.

In order to reach your full potential, you should begin a test with the proper mental attitude and a high degree of self-confidence. You should think of a test as an opportunity to document how much you know about the various tasks in your chosen profession. If you have been diligently studying the subject matter, you will be able to take your test in serenity because your mind will be well organized. If you are confident, you are more likely to do well because you have the proper mental attitude. If, on the other hand, your confidence is low, you are bound to do poorly. It is a self-fulfilling prophecy.

Perhaps you have heard athletic coaches talk about the importance of confidence when competing in sports. Mental confidence helps an athlete to perform at the highest level and gain an advantage over competitors. Taking a test is much like an athletic event. You are competing against yourself, in a certain sense, because you will be trying to approach perfection in determining your answers. As in any competition, you should aim your sights high and be confident that you can reach the apex.

Anxiety and Fear

Many technicians experience anxiety and fear at the very thought of taking a test. Many worry, become nervous, and even become ill at test time because of the fear of failure. Many often worry about the criticism and ridicule that may come from their employer, relatives, and peers. Some worry about taking a test because they feel that the stakes are very high. Those who spent a great amount of time studying may feel they must get a high grade to justify their efforts. The thought of not doing well can result in unnecessary worry. They become so worried, in fact, that their reasoning and thinking ability is impaired, actually bringing about the problem they wanted to avoid.

The fear of failure should not be confused with the desire for success. It is natural to become "psyched-up" for a test in contemplation of what is to come. A little emotion can provide a healthy flow of adrenaline to peak your senses and hone your mental ability. This improves your performance on the test and is a very different reaction from fear.

Most technician's fears and insecurities experienced before a test are due to a lack of self-confidence. Those who have not scored well on previous tests or have no confidence in their preparation are those most likely to fail. Be confident that you will do well on your test and your fears should vanish. You will know that you have done everything possible to realize your potential.

Getting Rid of Fear

If you have previously experienced fear of taking a test, it may be difficult to change your attitude immediately. It may be easier to cope with fear if you have a better understanding of what the test is about. A test is merely an assessment of how much the technician knows about a particular task area. Tests, then, are much less threatening when thought of in this manner. This does not mean, however, that you should lower your self-esteem simply because you performed poorly on a test.

You can consider the test essentially as a learning device, providing you with valuable information to evaluate your performance and knowledge. Recognize that no one is perfect. All humans make mistakes. The idea, then, is to make mistakes before the test, learn from them, and avoid repeating them on the test. Fortunately, this is not as difficult as it seems. Practical questions in this study guide include the correct answers to consider if you have made mistakes on the practice test. You should learn where you went wrong so you will not repeat them in the ASE test. If you learn from your mistakes, the stage is set for future growth.

If you understood everything presented up until now, you have the knowledge to become a test-wise technician, but more is required. To be a test-wise technician, you not only have to practice these principles, you have to diligently study in your task area.

Effective Study

The fundamental and vital requirement to induce effective study is a genuine and intense desire to achieve. This is more basic than any rule or technique that will be given here. The key requirement, then, is a driving motivation to learn and to achieve.

If you wish to study effectively, first develop a desire to master your studies and sincerely believe that you will master them. Everything else is secondary to such a desire.

First, build up definite ambitions and ideals toward which your studies can lead. Picture the satisfaction of success. The attitude of the technician may be transformed from merely getting by to an earnest and energetic effort. The best direct stimulus to change may involve nothing more than the deliberate planning of your time. Plan time to study.

Another drive that creates positive study is an interest in the subject studied. As an automotive technician, you can develop an interest in studying particular subjects if you follow these four rules:

1. Acquire information from a variety of sources. The greater your interest in a subject, the easier it is to learn about it. Visit your local library and seek books on the subject you are studying. When you find something new or of interest, make inexpensive photocopies for future study.

2. Merge new information with your previous knowledge. Discover the relationship of new facts to old known facts. Modern developments in automotive technology take on new interest when they are seen in relation to present knowledge.

3. Make new information personal. Relate the new information to matters that are of concern to you. The information you are now reading, for example, has interest to you as you think about how it can help.

4. Use your new knowledge. Raise questions about the points made by the book. Try to anticipate what the next steps and conclusions will be. Discuss this new knowledge, particularly the difficult and questionable points, with your peers.

You will find that when you study with eager interest, you will discover it is no longer work. It is pleasure and you will be fascinated in what you study. Studying can be like reading a novel or seeing a movie that overcomes distractions and requires no effort or willpower. You will discover that the positive relationship between interest and effort works both ways. Even though you perhaps began your studies with little or no interest, simply staying with it helped you to develop an interest in your studies.

Obviously, certain subject matter studies are bound to be of little or no interest, particularly in the beginning. Parts of certain studies may continue to be uninteresting. An honest effort to master those subjects, however, nearly always brings about some level of interest. If you appreciate the necessity and reward of effective studying, you will rarely be disappointed. Here are a few important hints for gaining the determination that is essential to carrying good conclusions into actual practice.

Make Study Definite

Decide what is to be studied and when it is to be studied. If the unit is discouragingly long, break it into two or more parts. Determine exactly what is involved in the first part and learn that. Only then should you proceed to the next part. Stick to a schedule.

The Urge to Learn

Make clear to yourself the relation of your present knowledge to your study materials. Determine the relevance with regard to your long-range goals and ambitions.

Turn your attention away from real or imagined difficulties as well as other things that you would rather be doing. Some major distractions are thoughts of other duties and of disturbing problems. These distractions can usually be put aside, simply shunted off by listing them in a notebook. Most technicians have found that by writing interfering thoughts down, their minds are freed from annoying tensions.

Adopt the most reasonable solution you can find or seek objective help from someone else for personal problems. Personal problems and worry are often causes of ineffective study. Sometimes there are no satisfactory solutions. Some manage to avoid the problems or to meet them without great worry. For those who may wish to find better ways of meeting their personal problems, the following suggestions are offered:

1. Determine as objectively and as definitely as possible where the problem lies. What changes are needed to remove the problem, and which changes, if any, can be made? Sometimes it is wiser to alter your goals than external conditions. If there is no perfect solution, explore the others. Some solutions may be better than others.

2. Seek an understanding confidant who may be able to help analyze and meet your problems. Very often, talking over your problems with someone in whom you have confidence and trust will help you to arrive at a solution.

3. Do not betray yourself by trying to evade the problem or by pretending that it has been solved. If social problem distractions prevent you from studying or doing satisfactory work, it is better to admit this to yourself. You can then decide what can be done about it.

Once you are free of interferences and irritations, it is much easier to stay focused on your studies.

Concentrate

To study effectively, you must concentrate. Your ability to concentrate is governed, to a great extent, by your surroundings as well as your physical condition. When absorbed in study, you must be oblivious to everything else around you. As you learn to concentrate and study, you must also learn to overcome all distractions. There are three kinds of distractions you may face:

1. Distractions in the surrounding area, such as motion, noise, and the glare of lights. The sun shining through a window on your study area, for example, can be very distracting.

   Some technicians find that, for effective study, it is necessary to eliminate visual distractions as well as noises. Others find that they are able to tolerate moderate levels of auditory or visual distraction.

   Make sure your study area is properly lighted and ventilated. The lighting should be adequate but should not shine directly into your eyes or be visible out of the corner of your eye. Also, try to avoid a reflection of the lighting on the pages of your book.

   Whether heated or cooled, the environment should be at a comfortable level. For most, this means a temperature of 78°F–80°F (25.6°C–26.7°C) with a relative humidity of 45 to 50 percent.

2. Distractions arising from your body, such as a headache, fatigue, and hunger. Be in good physical condition. Eat wholesome meals at regular times. Try to eat with your family or friends whenever possible. Mealtime should be your recreational period. Do not eat a heavy meal for lunch, and do not resume studies immediately after eating lunch. Just after lunch, try to get some regular exercise, relaxation, and recreation. A little exercise on a regular basis is much more valuable than a lot of exercise only on occasion.

3. Distractions of irrelevant ideas, such as how to repair the garden gate, when you are studying for an automotive-related test.

The problems associated with study are no small matter. These problems of distractions are generally best dealt with by a process of elimination. A few important rules for eliminating distractions follow.

Get Sufficient Sleep

You must get plenty of rest even if it means dropping certain outside activities. Avoid cutting in on your sleep time; you will be rewarded in the long run. If you experience difficulty going to sleep, do something to take your mind off your work and try to relax before going to bed. Some suggestions that may help include a little reading, a warm bath, a short walk, a conversation with a friend, or writing that overdue letter to a distant relative. If sleeplessness is an ongoing problem, consult a physician. Do not try any of the sleep remedies on the market, particularly if you are on medication, without approval of your physician.

If you still have difficulty studying, a final rule may help. Sit down in a favorable place for studying, open your books, and take out your pencil and paper. In a word, go through the motions.

Arrange Your Area

Arrange your chair and work area. To avoid strain and fatigue, whenever possible, shift your position occasionally. Try to be comfortable; however, avoid being too comfortable. It is nearly impossible to study rigorously when settled back in a large easy chair or reclining leisurely on a sofa.

When studying, it is essential to have a plan of action, a time to work, a time to study, and a time for pleasure. If you schedule your day and adhere to the schedule, you will eliminate most of your efforts and worries. A plan that is followed, then, soon becomes the easy and natural routine of the day. Most technicians find it useful to have a definite place and time to study. A particular table and chair should always be used for study and intellectual work. This place will then come to mean study. To be seated in that particular location at a regularly scheduled time will automatically lead you to assume a readiness for study.

Don't Daydream

Daydreaming or mind-wandering is an enemy of effective study. Daydreaming is frequently due to an inadequate understanding of words. Use the Glossary or a dictionary to look up the troublesome word. Another frequent cause of daydreaming is a deficient background in the present subject matter. When this is the problem, go back and review the subject matter to obtain the necessary foundation. Just one hour of concentrated study is equivalent to ten hours with frequent lapses of daydreaming. Be on guard against mind-wandering, and pull yourself back into focus on every occasion.

Study Regularly

A system of regularity in study is believed by many scholars to be the secret of success. The daily time schedule must, however, be determined on an individual basis. You must decide how many hours of each day you can devote to your studies. Few technicians really are aware of where their leisure time is spent. An accurate account of how your days are presently being spent is an important first step toward creating an effective daily schedule.

Weekly Schedule							
	Sun	Mon	Tues	Wed	Thu	Fri	Sat
6:00							
6:30							
7:00							
7:30							
8:00							
8:30							
9:00							
9:30							
10:00							
10:30							
11:00							
11:30							
NOON							
12:30							
1:00							
1:30							
2:00							
2:30							
3:00							
3:30							
4:00							
4:30							
5:00							
5:30							
6:00							
6:30							
7:00							
7:30							
8:00							
8:30							
9:00							
9:30							
10:00							
10:30							
11:00							
11:30							

The convenient form is for keeping an hourly record of your week's activities. If you fill in the schedule each evening before bedtime, you will soon gain some interesting and useful facts about yourself and your use of your time. If you think over the causes of wasted time, you can determine how you might better spend your time. A practical schedule can be set up by using the following steps.

1. Mark your fixed commitments, such as work, on your schedule. Be sure to include classes and clubs. Do you have sufficient time left? You can arrive at an estimate of the time you need for studying by counting the hours used during the present week. An often-used formula, if you are taking classes, is to multiply the number of hours you spend in class by two. This provides time for class studies. This is then added to your work hours. Do not forget time allocation for travel.

2. Fill in your schedule for meals and studying. Use as much time as you have available during the normal workday hours. Do not plan, for example, to do all of your studying between 11:00 P.M. and 1:00 A.M. Try to select a time for study that you can use every day without interruption. You may have to use two or perhaps three different study periods during the day.

3. List the things you need to do within a time period. A one-week time frame seems to work well for most technicians. The question you may ask yourself is: "What do I need to do to be able to walk into the test next week, or next month, prepared to pass?"

4. Break down each task into smaller tasks. The amount of time given to each area must also be settled. In what order will you tackle your schedule? It is best to plan the approximate time for your assignments and the order in which you will do them. In this way, you can avoid the difficulties of not knowing what to do first and of worrying about the other things you should be doing.

5. List your tasks in the empty spaces on your schedule. Keep some free time unscheduled so you can deal with any unexpected events, such as a dental appointment. You will then have a tentative schedule for the following week. It should be flexible enough to allow some units to be rearranged if necessary. Your schedule should allow time off from your studies. Some use the promise of a planned recreational period as a reward for motivating faithfulness to a schedule. You will more likely lose control of your schedule if it is packed too tightly.

Keep a Record

Keep a record of what you actually do. Use the knowledge you gain by keeping a record of what you are actually doing so you can create or modify a schedule for the following week. Be sure to give yourself credit for movement toward your goals and objectives. If you find that you cannot study productively at a particular hour, modify your schedule so as to correct that problem.

Scoring the ASE Test

You can gain a better perspective about tests if you know and understand how they are scored. ASE's tests are scored by American College Testing (ACT), a nonpartial, nonbiased organization having no vested interest in ASE or in the automotive industry. Each question carries the same weight as any other question. For example, if there are fifty questions, each is worth 2 percent of the total score. The passing grade is 70 percent. That means you must correctly answer thirty-five of the fifty questions to pass the test.

Understand the Test Results

The test results can tell you:

- where your knowledge equals or exceeds that needed for competent performance, or
- where you might need more preparation.

The test results *cannot* tell you:

- how you compare with other technicians, or
- how many questions you answered correctly.

Your ASE test score report will show the number of correct answers you got in each of the content areas. These numbers provide information about your performance in each area of the test. However, because there may be a different number of questions in each area of the test, a high percentage of correct answers in an area with few questions may not offset a low percentage in an area with many questions.

It may be noted that one does not "fail" an ASE test. The technician that does not pass is simply told "More Preparation Needed." Though large differences in percentages may indicate problem areas, it is important to consider how many questions were asked in each area. Since each test evaluates all phases of the work involved in a service specialty, you should be prepared in each area. A low score in one area could keep you from passing an entire test.

Note that a typical test will contain the number of questions indicated above each content area's description. For example:

Heating, Ventilation, and Air Conditioning (HVAC) Systems (Test T7)

Content Area	Questions	Percent of Test
A. HVAC Systems Diagnosis, Service, and Repair	8	20%
B. A/C System and Component Diagnosis, Service, and Repair	14	35%
1. A/C System - General (5)		
2. Compressor and Clutch (4)		
3. Evaporator, Condenser, and Related Components (5)		
C. Heating and Engine Cooling Systems Diagnosis, Service, and Repair	6	15%
D. Operating Systems and Related Controls Diagnosis and Repair	8	20%
1. Electrical (5)		
2. Air/Vacuum/Mechanical (2)		
3. Automatic Temperature Control (1)		
E. Refrigerant Recovery, Recycling, and Handling	4	10%
Total	*40	100%

*__Note:__ *The test could contain up to ten additional questions that are included for statistical research purposes only. Your answers to these questions will not affect your score, but since you do not know which ones they are, you should answer all questions in the test. The five-year Recertification Test will cover the same content areas as those listed above. However, the number of questions in each content area of the Recertification Test will be reduced by about one-half.*

"Average"

There is no such thing as average. You cannot determine your overall test score by adding the percentages given for each task area and dividing by the number of areas. It doesn't work that way because there generally are not the same number of questions in each task area. A task area with twenty questions, for example, counts more toward your total score than a task area with ten questions.

So, How Did You Do?

Your test report should give you a good picture of your results and a better understanding of your task areas of strength and weakness.

If you fail to pass the test, you may take it again at any time it is scheduled to be administered. You are the only one who will receive your test score. Test scores will not be given over the telephone by ASE nor will they be released to anyone without your written permission.

Are You Sure You're Ready for Test T7?

Pretest

The purpose of this pretest is to determine the amount of review that you may require prior to taking the ASE Medium/Heavy Truck Test: Heating, Ventilation, and Air Conditioning (HVAC) Systems (Test T7). If you answer all of the pretest questions correctly, complete the sample test in section 5 along with the additional test questions in section 6.

If two or more of your answers to the pretest questions are wrong, study section 4: An Overview of the System before continuing with the sample test and additional test questions.

The pretest answers and explanations are located at the end of the pretest.

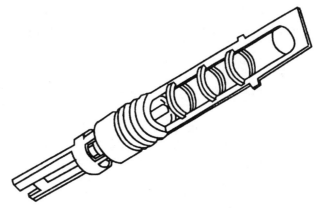

1. A technician finds the component shown in the figure above clogged. Which of these conditions will result?
   A. Frost on the receiver/dryer
   B. High high-side pressure
   C. Low high-side pressure
   D. Bubbles in the sight glass

2. All of the following are true statements **EXCEPT:**
   A. refrigerant leaves the compressor as a high-pressure gas.
   B. refrigerant enters the orifice tube as a high-pressure liquid.
   C. refrigerant leaves the evaporator as a low-pressure gas.
   D. refrigerant leaves the condenser as a low-pressure liquid.

3. What is the refrigerant currently used in mobile A/C systems?
   A. R-12
   B. R-134a
   C. Ammonia
   D. R-11

4. What color(s) do the SAE specification state that R-134a service hoses for the high side of the system will be?
   A. Solid red
   B. Solid blue with a black stripe
   C. Solid black with a yellow stripe
   D. Solid red with a black stripe

5. A customer complains that his windshield fogs up. Technician A says a plugged evaporator drain can cause windshield fogging. Technician B says that a leaking heater core can be the cause. Who is right?
   A. Technician A only
   B. Technician B only
   C. Both A and B
   D. Neither A nor B

6. The evaporator fins in a cycling-clutch type air conditioning system freeze up regardless of the temperature control setting. Technician A says the system is overcharged. Technician B says the thermostatic switch is stuck closed. Who is right?
   A. Technician A only
   B. Technician B only
   C. Both A and B
   D. Neither A nor B

7. When pressure testing a cooling system, there are no obvious leaks but the system cannot maintain pressure. The most likely cause of this problem is:
   A. a leaking evaporator.
   B. a blown head gasket in the engine.
   C. a leaking power steering cooler.
   D. a leaking transmission oil cooler.

8. With the selector lever in the MAX A/C position, a blend air HVAC system outputs cold air for about 15 minutes, at which time the output air becomes warm. The most likely cause of this problem is:
   A. a defective coolant control valve.
   B. a defective blend air door return spring.
   C. a defective thermal-expansion valve.
   D. a defective fresh air door.

9. A customer complains of poor heater performance on a "blend air" type HVAC system. All of these could cause this problem **EXCEPT:**
   A. vacuum circuit to water valve.
   B. cable adjustment.
   C. wrong thermostat.
   D. low coolant level.

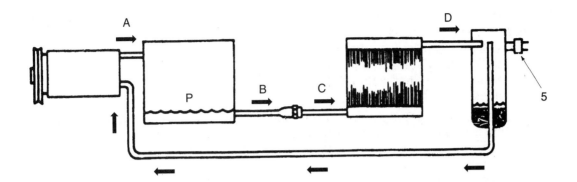

10. The purpose of the refrigerant system component 5, shown in the figure above, is to which of the following functions?
    A. protect system components from excessive pressure.
    B. cycle the compressor on and off in relation to system pressure.
    C. shut off the compressor if the refrigerant charge is low.
    D. shut off the compressor if the refrigerant temperature is high.

11. The A/C compressor clutch will not engage. What is the LEAST likely cause of this problem?
    A. The A/C system refrigerant charge is one-half pound low.
    B. The A/C system is empty.
    C. There is an open circuit in the binary switch.
    D. There is an open circuit in the compressor clutch coil.

12. What is the LEAST likely reason that a blower motor will not run?
    A. A low refrigerant charge
    B. A blown fuse
    C. An open resistor
    D. A defective switch

Answers to the Test Questions for the Pretest

1. C, 2. D, 3. B, 4. D, 5. C, 6. B, 7. B, 8. C, 9. A, 10. B, 11. A, 12. A

Explanations to the Answers for the Pretest

Question #1
Answer A is wrong. The component shown is an orifice tube and a restriction in the receiver/drier will cause frost forming on that component.
Answer B is wrong. If there is serious restriction in the gas flow, high pressure cannot be generated.
Answer C is correct. A restriction or clogging at the orifice tube will cause low low-side and low high-side pressure on a manifold gauge set. The compressor cannot suck in enough gas to create any pressure.
Answer D is wrong. Air entering the system from a low refrigerant charge causes bubbles in the sight glass if the system uses a sight glass (typically clutch orifice tube systems do not use a sight glass).

Question #2
Answer A is wrong. Refrigerant does leave the compressor as a high-pressure gas.
Answer B is wrong. Refrigerant enters the orifice tube as a high-pressure liquid.
Answer C is wrong. Refrigerant does leave the evaporator as a low-pressure gas.
Answer D is correct. Refrigerant does not leave the condenser as a low-pressure liquid. It leaves the condenser as a high-pressure liquid.

Question #3
Answer A is wrong. R-12 is not currently used in mobile air conditioner production.
Answer B is correct. R-134a is the refrigerant currently used in mobile A/C systems.
Answer C is wrong. Dry nitrogen gas is usually recommended for purging A/C systems of damp air, traces of refrigerant, and loose dirt.
Answer D is wrong. R-11 was an early flushing agent, it is no longer in use.

Question #4
Answer A is wrong. The color is not solid red, but solid red with a black stripe.
Answer B is wrong. The color is solid red, not solid blue.
Answer C is wrong. The color is solid red, not solid black.
Answer D is correct. The color is solid red with a black stripe.

Question #5
Answer A is wrong. A plugged evaporator case drain will cause windshield fogging due to retained moisture, but the answer choice is wrong because both technicians are correct.
Answer B is wrong. A leaking radiator core also results in retained moisture, but the answer choice is wrong because both technicians are correct.
Answer C is correct. Fogging of the windshield can be caused by a plugged evaporator case drain, a leaking heater core, a loose hose to core connection, or water (from rain or washing,) entering the evaporator/heater core case.
Answer D is wrong. Both technicians are correct.

Question #6
Answer A is wrong. An overcharged system cycles off and on constantly and results in low cooling because it can pull down the pressure.
Answer B is correct. When the thermostatic switch sticks closed, the compressor clutch will not cycle resulting in evaporator fins freezing.
Answer C is wrong. Only technician B is correct.
Answer D is wrong. Only technician B is correct.

Question #7
Answer A is wrong. The evaporator is a component of the A/C system and not related to engine overheating.
Answer B is correct. With no external leaks, a blown head gasket will leak coolant internally into the combustion chamber and be consumed by the engine. It is the most likely cause of an internal leak.
Answer C is wrong. A leaking power steering cooler is the least likely cause of the distracters and a visible external leak source.
Answer D is wrong. If the transmission cooler was leaking there would be an intermix of coolant with transmission fluid and the radiator contents would resemble a strawberry milk shake.

Question #8
Answer A is wrong. A defective coolant flow control would cause a low cooling condition at all times, therefore this is a highly unlikely cause.
Answer B is wrong. The blend door controls the position of the air not the temperature, therefore this is a least likely cause.
Answer C is correct. An expansion valve when sticking, will exhibit these characteristics, therefore this is the most likely cause.
Answer D is wrong. The fresh-air door would not change in a fifteen-minute interval.

Question #9
Answer A is correct. Blend air type HVAC systems do not use a hot-water valve. Improper blend door cable adjustment, the wrong thermostat, or low-coolant level can cause poor heater performance in blend air systems.
Answer B is wrong. Cable adjustment can be the cause of poor heater performance.
Answer C is wrong. The wrong thermostat can cause poor cold engine-heater performance.
Answer D is wrong. Low coolant level contributes to poor heater performance.

Question #10
Answer A is wrong. The high-pressure cutoff switch would perform that function and this component turns off the compressor at 25 psi and turns it on at 46 psi. It stays on above 46 psi.
Answer B is correct. The component asked for in the figure is the pressure-cycling switch. This component cycles the compressor clutch on and off in relation to refrigerant pressure to prevent evaporator freezing.
Answer C is wrong. The pressure-cycling switch will not shutoff the compressor with low refrigerant unless the pressure drops to less than 25 psi.
Answer D is wrong. This component does not directly measure temperature except through the Charles Constant Volume Law that shows temperature increases in relation to increases at a constant volume.

Question #11
Answer A is correct. The loss of one-half pound of refrigerant will not prevent the compressor clutch from engaging. An empty system or open circuits in the binary switch or coil will prevent clutch engagement.
Answer B is wrong. If the system was empty of refrigerant that would be a most likely cause if the compressor was not engaging due to open pressure switches.
Answer C is wrong. An open circuit in the binary switch will prevent compressor clutch operation.
Answer D is wrong. An open clutch coil results in no compressor operation.

Question #12
Answer A is correct. There is no direct connection between the blower motor operation and a low refrigerant charge on a non-ATC system.
Answer B is wrong. A blown fuse will cause no blower operation.
Answer C is wrong. An open resistor affects blower operation.
Answer D is wrong. A defective blower switch will cause the blower not to run.

Types of Questions

ASE certification tests are often thought of as being tricky. They may seem to be tricky if you do not completely understand what is being asked. The following examples will help you recognize certain types of ASE questions and avoid common errors.

Each test is made up of forty to eighty multiple-choice questions. Multiple-choice questions are an efficient way to test knowledge. To answer them correctly, you must think about each choice as a possibility, and then choose the one that best answers the question. To do this, read each word of the question carefully. Do not assume you know what the question is about until you have finished reading it.

Multiple-Choice Questions

One type of multiple-choice question has three wrong answers and one correct answer. The wrong answers, however, may be almost correct, so be careful not to jump at the first answer that seems to be correct. If all the answers seem to be correct, choose the answer that is the most correct. If you readily know the answer, this kind of question does not present a problem. If you are unsure of the answer, analyze the question and the answers. For example:

Question 1:

The water pump should be replaced any time:
A. the fan clutch is replaced.
B. the heater hoses are replaced.
C. there is a small leak from the weep hole.
D. the thermostat sticks closed.

Analysis:

Answer A is wrong because fan clutch replacement does not affect the life of the water pump.

Answer B is wrong because the water pump generally has a longer service life than the heater hoses.

Answer C is correct because even a small leak from the weep hole indicates that the front seal of the water pump has failed.

Answer D is wrong because thermostat operation does not indicate a need to replace the water pump.

EXCEPT Questions

Another type of question used on ASE tests has answers that are all correct except one. The correct answer for this type of question is the answer that is wrong. The word "EXCEPT" will always be in capital letters. You must identify which of the choices is the wrong answer. If you read quickly through the question, you may overlook what the question is asking and answer the question with the first correct statement. This will make your answer wrong. An example of this type of question and the analysis is as follows:

Question 2:

A/C compressor drive belt edge wear could indicate any of the following conditions **EXCEPT:**

A. a bent or cracked compressor mounting bracket.

B. improperly set compressor clutch air gap.

C. a damaged compressor pulley.

D. a worn idler pulley bearing.

Analysis:

Answer A is wrong because a cracked or bent mounting bracket can cause drive belt edge wear.

Answer B is correct because compressor clutch air gap does not affect pulley alignment.

Answer C is wrong because a damaged compressor pulley could cause drive belt edge wear.

Answer D is wrong because a worn idler pulley bearing could cause belt misalignment and result in edge wear.

Technician A, Technician B Questions

The type of question that is most popularly associated with an ASE test is the "Technician A says. . . . Technician B says. . . . Who is right?" type. In this type of question, you must identify the correct statement or statements. To answer this type of question correctly, you must carefully read each technician's statement and judge it on its own merit to determine if the statement is true.

Typically, this type of question begins with a statement about some analysis or repair procedure. This is followed by two statements about the cause of the problem, proper inspection, identification, or repair choices. You are asked whether the first statement, the second statement, both statements, or neither statement is correct. Analyzing this type of question is a little easier than the other types because there are only two ideas to consider although there are still four choices for an answer.

Technician A. . . . Technician B questions are really double-true-false questions. The best way to analyze this kind of question is to consider each technician's statement separately. Ask yourself, is A true or false? Is B true or false? Then select your answer from the four choices. An important point to remember is that an ASE Technician A. . . . Technician B question will never have Technician A and B directly disagreeing with each other. That is why you must evaluate each statement independently. An example of this type of question and the analysis of it follows.

Question 3:

Technician A says that when installing new A/C hose O-rings, a seal pick should be used to minimize skin contact with the new seal. Technician B says that the petroleum jelly used to lubricate the new O-rings will protect them from the oils in the skin. Who is right?

A. Technician A only

B. Technician B only

C. Both A and B

D. Neither A nor B

Analysis:

Answer A is wrong because a seal pick should never be used to install A/C hose O-rings.

Answer B is wrong because refrigeration oil is the only acceptable lubricant for A/C system O-rings and seals.

Answer C is wrong because both technicians are wrong.

Answer D is correct because neither technician is right.

Questions with a Figure

About 10 percent of ASE questions will have a figure, as shown in the following example:
Question 4:

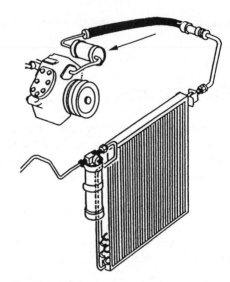

The arrow shown in the figure above is pointing to the:
A. pilot operated absolute (POA) valve.
B. filter.
C. evaporator temperature regulator (ETR).
D. muffler.

   Analysis:
Answer A is wrong because the POA valve is located near the evaporator.
Answer B is wrong because a filter is generally used on the suction side of the compressor.
Answer C is wrong because the ETR is located near the evaporator.
Answer D is correct because the indicated component is a muffler used to reduce compressor noise.

Most-Likely Questions

Most-likely questions are somewhat difficult because only one choice is correct while the other three choices are nearly correct. An example of a most-likely-cause question is as follows:

Question 5:
   In an ATC system, a grinding noise comes from under the dash when the temperature setting is changed from WARM to COLD. The most likely cause of this problem is:
A. grit in the evaporator case.
B. a faulty mode door actuator.
C. bad drive gears in the blend door motor.
D. arcing in the control head.

Analysis:

Answer A is wrong because grit in the evaporator case is not likely to cause this symptom.

Answer B is wrong because the mode door does not move when the temperature setting is changed.

Answer C is correct because bad drive gears in the blend door motor will cause this symptom.

Answer D is wrong because arcing in the control head will not cause a grinding noise.

LEAST-Likely Questions

Notice that in most-likely questions there is no capitalization. This is not so with least-likely type questions. For this type of question, look for the choice that would be the least likely cause of the described situation. Read the entire question carefully before choosing your answer. An example is as follows:

Question 6:

Which of the following is the LEAST likely cause of a shutter system that will not close completely?

A. A blown shutter fuse
B. An air leak in the hose to the shutter cylinder
C. Dirt accumulation on the shutter linkage
D. Ice build-up on the shutters

Analysis:

Answer A is correct because most shutter systems are air operated, not electrically operated.

Answer B is wrong because an air leak could cause the shutters to remain open.

Answer C is wrong because dirt accumulation on the shutter linkage could prevent the shutters from closing completely.

Answer D is wrong because ice build-up could prevent the shutters from closing completely.

Summary

There are no four-part multiple-choice ASE questions having "none of the above" or "all of the above" choices. ASE does not use other types of questions, such as fill-in-the-blank, completion, true-false, word-matching, or essay. ASE does not require you to draw diagrams or sketches. If a formula or chart is required to answer a question, it is provided for you. There are no ASE questions that require you to use a pocket calculator.

Testing Time Length

An ASE test session is four hours and fifteen minutes. You may attempt from one to a maximum of four tests in one session. It is recommended, however, that no more than a total of 225 questions be attempted at any test session. This will allow for just over one minute for each question.

Visitors are not permitted at any time. If you wish to leave the test room, for any reason, you must first ask permission. If you finish your test early and wish to leave, you are permitted to do so only during specified dismissal periods.

Monitor Your Progress

You should monitor your progress and set an arbitrary limit to how much time you will need for each question. This should be based on the number of questions you are attempting. It is suggested that you wear a watch because some facilities may not have a clock visible to all areas of the room.

Registration

Test centers are assigned on a first-come, first-served basis. To register for an ASE certification test, you should enroll at least six weeks before the scheduled test date. This should provide sufficient time to assure you a spot in the test center. It should also give you enough time for study in preparation for the test. Test sessions are offered by ASE twice each year, in May and November, at over six hundred sites across the United States. Some tests that relate to emission testing also are given in August in several states.

To register, contact Automotive Service Excellence/American College Testing at:

ASE/ACT
P.O. Box 4007
Iowa City, IA 52243

4 An Overview of the System

Heating, Ventilation, and Air Conditioning (HVAC) Systems (Test T7)

The following section includes the task areas and task lists for this test and a written overview of the topics covered in the test.

The task list describes the actual work you should be able to do as a technician that you will be tested on by the ASE. This is your key to the test and you should review this section carefully. We have based our sample test and additional questions upon these tasks, and the overview section will also support your understanding of the task list. ASE advises that the questions on the test may not equal the number of tasks listed; the task lists tell you what ASE expects you to know how to do and be ready to be tested on.

At the end of each question in the Sample Test and Additional Test Questions sections, a letter and number will be used as a reference back to this section for additional study. Note the following example: **A1**

Task List

A. HVAC System Diagnosis, Service, and Repair (8 Questions)

Task A1   Verify the need for service or repair of HVAC systems based on unusual operating noises; determine appropriate action.

1. An air conditioning (A/C) compressor has a growling noise only when the compressor clutch is engaged. Which of these could be the cause?
   A. A defective internal compressor bearing
   B. A defective pulley bearing
   C. A low refrigerant charge
   D. Excessive refrigerant system pressure   (A1)

Question #1
Answer A is correct. A defective internal compressor bearing causes a growling noise only when the clutch is engaged, since this is the only time the internal components are rotating.
Answer B is wrong. A defective pulley would make the growling noise when the clutch was engaged or disengaged.
Answer C is wrong. A low refrigerant charge will not cause a growling noise.
Answer D is wrong. Excessive refrigerant pressures cause thumping and heavy knocking type noises from the compressor, not a growling noise.

Task List and Overview

A. HVAC System Diagnosis, Service, and Repair
(8 Questions)

Task A1   **Verify the need for service or repair of HVAC systems based on unusual operating noises; determine appropriate action.**

The service technician must be aware of normal HVAC system operating noises in order to determine whether a system requires service. Normal noises include the sounds of A/C compressor clutch engagement, the blower motor, moving blend air and mode doors, and pressure equalization after the vehicle is shut down. Noises that could indicate the need for service include a growling sound from the water pump or A/C compressor, a whistling noise under the dash, and a grinding noise when control levers are moved.

A loose, dry, or worn A/C compressor belt will cause a squealing noise. This noise will be worse during acceleration. Worn or dry blower motor bearings may cause a squealing noise when the blower is running; this noise will occur when the engine first starts after the truck has sat overnight. A loose or worn clutch hub or loose compressor mounting bolt will also cause a rattling noise from the compressor.

If liquid refrigerant enters the compressor, a thumping, banging noise will result. Heavy knocking compressor noises come from the following: refrigerant system blockage, incorrect pressures, or internal damage. A worn compressor pulley bearing or air clutch bearing will cause a growling noise with the compressor engaged or disengaged. If the growling noise only occurs when the system engages the clutch, internal bearings may be at fault.

Task A2   **Verify the need for service or repair of HVAC systems based on unusual visual, smell, and touch conditions; determine appropriate action.**

The service technician must be aware of abnormal conditions in the HVAC system in order to determine the need for system service. If the driver complains of high or low temperatures inside the cab, this is cause for a system performance test. Abnormal conditions include the smell of anti-freeze inside the cab, a fogged windshield, ice build-up on A/C components, and oil or dirt build-up on A/C fittings.

Task A3   **Identify system type and conduct performance test(s) on HVAC systems; determine appropriate action.**

First, the technician must know if the system operates on R-12 or R-134a refrigerant. Most major R-134a components use a light-blue label to indicate an R-134a design. R-12 systems use Schrader type service valves, where R-134a systems use metric threads to quickly connect service valves.

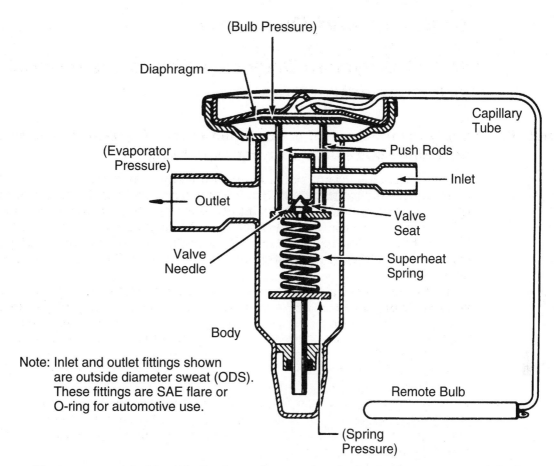

Note: Inlet and outlet fittings shown are outside diameter sweat (ODS). These fittings are SAE flare or O-ring for automotive use.

Next, you need to identify the type of expansion device in the evaporator inlet line. Most A/C systems use a thermal expansion valve (TXV) as shown in the figure above, or a fixed orifice tube (FOT) in the evaporator inlet line to control refrigerant flow into the evaporator. You have high-pressure liquid on the inlet side of the expansion device and low-pressure liquid on the outlet side. Other systems use a suction throttling device (STD) between the evaporator and the suction side of the compressor to control refrigerant flow into the evaporator. These suction throttling devices may include: a suction throttling valve (STV), pilot-operated absolute valve (POA), evaporator pressure regulator (EPR) valve, or an evaporator temperature regulator (ETR) valve. Many A/C systems use combination valves that usually contain two of the pressure-control valves. For example, older GM class 8 tractors used an evaporator equalized valves-in-receiver (EE-VIR) assembly that contains TXV and POA valves plus a receiver dryer. Some Ford trucks have a combination valve containing a TXV and STV. Mack trucks use a block-type assembly that contains an equalized TXV.

The truck industry uses three types of A/C systems: mechanical, semiautomatic, or automatic. Mechanical systems use a slide-type lever or rotary switch to control the in-cab temperature manually. In a semiautomatic system, a computer electronically controls some systems and in the automatic systems, most sub-systems are computer controlled.

Manual systems rely on the driver to select the temperature, mode, and blower speed. Semiautomatic temperature control (SATC) systems regulate only the temperature of the output air and rely on the driver to select the desired mode and blower speed. A microprocessor (computer) controls a fully automatic temperature control (ATC) system. These systems use the input from various sensors throughout the vehicle to control the blend doors automatically to adjust the interior temperature using an appropriate blower speed.

An HVAC performance test should include operation of the system in all modes, and at a variety of temperatures and blower speeds. A small, pocket thermometer should be used to verify that the output air temperatures match the temperature settings.

B. A/C System and Component Diagnosis, Service, and Repair (14 Questions)

1. A/C System—General (5 Questions)

Task B1.1 Diagnose the cause of temperature control problems in the A/C system; determine needed repairs.

The temperature of A/C system output air is generally controlled by one of two ways. In blend air systems, air cooled by the evaporator core is mixed with air warmed by the heater core. Ultimately, the output air temperature control occurs by regulating the amount of air allowed to flow through each core. In other A/C systems, temperature control is achieved by cycling the compressor clutch. The compressor-clutch cycling rate is usually controlled by the engine control module or the body control module based on input from various temperature sensors.

A/C system output air temperature is affected by outside air temperature and humidity, engine coolant temperature, air flow through the condenser and evaporator, and level of refrigerant charge. Output air temperature may also be affected by mechanical or electrical failure of system components.

Task B1.2 Identify refrigerant type.

The easiest way to identify the type of refrigerant that is used in a given A/C system is to observe the service fittings. Society of Automotive Engineers (SAE) standard J639 defines the size and type of service fittings for R-12 and R-134a A/C systems. R-12 service fittings have external threads. R-134a systems use quick-disconnect fittings. You cannot vent either R-12 or R-134a to the atmosphere.

Task B1.3 Diagnose A/C system problems indicated by pressure gauge readings and sight glass/moisture indicator conditions (where applicable); determine needed service or repairs.

In a normally operating A/C system, the low-side pressure varies between 20 and 45 psi, and the high-side pressure varies between 120 and 210 psi. The following table summarizes abnormal A/C system pressures and common causes.

A/C Pressure Diagnosis

LOW-SIDE PRESSURE	HIGH-SIDE PRESSURE	POSSIBLE CAUSES
LOW	LOW	Low refrigerant charge
LOW	LOW	Obstruction in the suction line
LOW	LOW	Clogged orifice tube
LOW	LOW	TXV valve stuck closed*
LOW	LOW	Restricted line from the condenser to the evaporator*
LOW	HIGH	Restricted evaporator air flow
HIGH	LOW	Internal compressor damage
HIGH	HIGH	Refrigerant overcharge
HIGH	HIGH	Restricted condenser air flow
HIGH	HIGH	High engine coolant temperature
HIGH	HIGH	TXV valve stuck open
HIGH	HIGH	Air or moisture in the refrigerant

*Stuck closed TXV valves or a restricted line from the condenser to the evaporator will cause frosting at the point of restriction.

In some A/C systems, a sight glass allows the service technician to make a quick assessment of the system condition. With the A/C compressor clutch engaged, a properly charged system will occasionally show traces of bubbles. A sight glass that appears foamy indicates that the refrigerant charge is low. When the sight glass contains bubbles and/or foam, the refrigerant charge is low and air has entered the system. Oil streaks appearing in the sight glass indicate that compressor oil is circulating through the system. A cloudy sight glass indicates that the desiccant bag in the receiver/drier has broken down.

On R-12 systems, sight glass indications are only valid when the ambient (surrounding area) temperature is above 71°F (21°C). If the temperature is below 70°F, it is normal for bubbles to appear in the sight glass. A clear sight glass may indicate the proper refrigerant charge. A sight glass may also indicate an excessive refrigerant charge, or no refrigerant charge. Many R-134a systems do not have a sight glass. Most manufacturers agree that the following conditions must be present when diagnosing an R-134a system:

- high side below 240 psi (1570 kPa)
- ambient temperature below 95°F (35°C)
- temperature control set in the lowest position
- humidity below 70 percent
- high blower speed
- engine speed set at 1500 RPM
- recirculation air set

R-134a systems have a normal charge if the sight glass shows a stream of very small bubbles that disappear when the engine speed is increased. On an R-134a system, when the sight glass shows no bubbles, the system is overcharged. A constant flow of bubbles mixed with foam indicates a low charge. If the refrigerant charge is very low, fog may appear in the sight glass. R-12 mineral oil in an R-134a system causes a severely fogged sight glass.

Task B1.4 Diagnose A/C system problems indicated by visual, smell, and touch procedures; determine needed repairs.

To diagnose A/C systems efficiently, the service technician must use all of his senses. Restricted hoses cause a frosting or sudden temperature change at a specific point along the hose. Frost on the receiver/dryer usually indicates an internal restriction in that component. Because the receiver/dryer is located in the high-pressure liquid line between the condenser and evaporator, it should feel warm. TXV valve frosting indicates a restricted valve or one sticking closed. Frost formation on the evaporator outlet indicates a flooded evaporator, caused by an excessive refrigerant charge, or a stuck open TXV valve. Unusual noises can often guide the technician to a faulty component. These problems may also cause frost on the compressor suction line. On a system that uses a POA valve, frosting of the suction line is normal.

On systems using an accumulator, it should feel cold because of its close connection to the evaporator. Both the evaporator inlet and outlet should feel cold, when operating normally. On orifice tube systems, the evaporator inlet should be slightly warmer to the touch than the outlet. If the evaporator outlet is warm, the refrigerant charge may be low. High-side refrigerant components should feel hot or warm, and low-side components should feel cool or cold. A plugged drain in the evaporator case causes a strong rotten egg smell in the cab.

A thorough visual inspection is always a good first step in diagnosing A/C systems.

Task B1.5 Perform A/C system leak test; determine needed repairs.

Refrigerant systems use the following two methods to detect leaks: dye check or electronic leak detector. To check an A/C system for leaks, the technician must first ensure that the system contains enough refrigerant to allow compressor clutch engagement. If the system is empty, install a partial refrigerant charge. On an R-12 system, you can use a special R-12 that contains a dye. After running with the dye installed for 15 minutes, the dye will appear at the leak area. Ultraviolet dye is available for installation into the refrigerant and visible under a black light detector. Electronic detectors provide an audible beeping sound when the probe is placed near the leak source. Since R-12 and R-134a are different chemically, a specific electronic detector or one that does both systems is used. When checking for leaks, place the leak detector probe directly below each fitting and each component, directly below the evaporator drain, and at the center panel duct. Check the entire system to rule out multiple leaks.

When using an electronic leak detector, calibrate the detector before each use. When using a flame-type leak detector, light the torch and warm the reaction plate until it glows red, then adjust the flame until it burns pale blue. Watch the flame while moving the search hose. If a small leak is found, the flame becomes light green to yellow. A large leak causes a purple flame.

Task B1.6 Evacuate A/C system using appropriate equipment.

When evacuating an A/C system, it is important to follow the manufacturer's instructions for the specific recovery station used. Never vent refrigerant to the atmosphere; it is an illegal and environmentally irresponsible action.

When the system is completely empty, connect the manifold gauge center hose to a vacuum pump. Operate this pump for 30 minutes with the service valves open and the low-side gauge valve open. After 5 minutes of operation, the low-side gauge should indicate 20 in. Hg. (67.6 kPa), and the high-side should read below zero, unless it is restricted by a stop pin. If the high-side gauge does not drop below zero, this indicates refrigerant blockage. When the technician finds blockage, he must fix this first before proceeding with the evacuation process. After 15 minutes of evacuation, the low-side should indicate 24 to 26 in. Hg. (81–88 kPa), if there are no leaks. If less than this valve is found, close the low-side gauge valve and observe the gauge. If the low-side gauge needle rises slowly, this indicates a refrigerant leak. Fix the leak and proceed and evacuate the system to at least 27 in. Hg. Most manufacturers recommend that the vacuum pump run for at least
30 minutes to ensure that you remove all moisture from the system is removed.

Task B1.7 Internally clean A/C system components and hoses.

If desiccant bag deterioration or catastrophic compressor failure occurs, clean all refrigeration system components internally. Internal cleaning of A/C system components is best accomplished by flushing with nitrogen. Before flushing, the compressor and all restricting components and filters must be removed from the system. It is important to regulate the pressure from the nitrogen supply tank to normal system pressure for each component.

Rather than system flushing, many truck manufacturers recommend using an in-line filter between the condenser and the evaporator to remove debris. These in-line filters come with or without FOT. If you use the filter that contains a FOT, you must remove the other FOT from the system.

Task B1.8 Charge A/C system with refrigerant.

The technician must complete the recovery and evacuation procedure before charging a refrigerant system. Modern recovery and charging stations do not require the A/C system to operate during system charging. It is always best to read all of the manufacturer's instructions for the specific charging station used. The original equipment manufacturer (OEM) may recommend high-side (liquid) or low-side (vapor) charging procedures. You must close both the high-side and low-side manifold gauge valves.

Connect the center hose to the proper refrigerant container and open the container valve. With the engine not running, using the high-side (liquid) charging process, open the high-side gauge valve and observe the low-side gauge, then close the high-side gauge. If the low-side gauge does not move from a vacuum to a pressure, the refrigerant system is restricted. With no restriction present, open the high-side gauge valve to proceed with the high-side (liquid) charging procedure. Charging is complete when the correct weight of refrigerant has entered the system. Turn the compressor over by hand to make sure that no liquid refrigerant is in the compressor. Now start the engine and run an A/C performance test.

Task B1.9 Identify lubricant type.

All R-12 systems use mineral-based refrigeration oil to lubricate the compressor and prevent internal corrosion of components. Mineral-based oil is not compatible with R-134a systems. R-134a systems use Polyalkylene Glycol (PAG)-based refrigeration oil. The PAG lubricant is synthetic oil and is not compatible with R-12 systems.

2. Compressor and Clutch (4 Questions)

Task B2.1 Diagnose A/C system problems that cause protection devices (pressure, thermal, and electronic) to interrupt system operation; determine needed repairs.

A variety of A/C system protection devices can be used in mobile A/C systems. The low pressure cut-out switch will interrupt compressor operation if system pressure drops to the point that a loss of refrigerant charge occurs. The high-pressure cut-out switch interrupts compressor operation in case of extremely high system pressure. The binary switch combines the function of the low and high pressure cut-out switches. Some systems have a high-pressure relief valve mounted in the receiver/dryer. This valve opens and relieves system pressure if the pressure exceeds 450 to 550 psi (3100 to 3792 kPa). Condenser air flow restrictions cause these extremely high pressures. In gasoline and diesel engine electronic fuel management systems, the computer operates a relay that supplies voltage to the compressor clutch. All input signals go to the engine computer. In some applications, this includes a refrigerant pressure signal. If this input signals an abnormal low or high pressure condition, the engine computer will not engage the compressor.

Cycling clutch orifice tube (CCOT) systems use a pressure cycling switch to cycle the compressor off and on, in relation to low-side pressure. This switch is mounted in the accumulator between the evaporator and the compressor. This switch closes and turns on the compressor when the refrigerant pressure is above 46 psi (315 kPa). The dash A/C switch supplies the power to the cycling switch. The pressure switch opens when the system pressure decreases to 25 psi (175 kPa). This cycling action maintains the evaporator temperature at 33°F (1°C).

Some refrigerant systems use a thermostatic clutch cycling switch that cycles the compressor on and off in relation to evaporator outlet temperature.

Task B2.2 Inspect, test, and replace A/C system pressure, thermal, and electronic protection devices.

A/C system protection pressure switches are normally closed. Most of these switches are mounted on Schrader valves to facilitate replacement without the need to evacuate and recharge the system.

Task B2.3 Inspect, adjust, and replace A/C compressor drive belts and pulleys.

When inspecting an A/C system, it is important that the technician not overlook the A/C compressor drive belts and pulleys. Drive belt edge wear indicates a misaligned or bent pulley. If the belt is loose or bottomed out in the pulley, the belt may slip and cause inadequate cooling. Cracked or frayed belts must be replaced. Use a standard drive belt tension to check and adjust belt tension. An improperly adjusted drive belt will wear or fail prematurely. A drive belt adjusted too loosely may slip and cause belt squealing, especially on acceleration with the A/C on and clutch engaged. A drive belt adjusted too tightly may cause internal engine wear or damage to other belt-driven components. One must replace, not repair, cracked or bent pulleys.

Task B2.4 Inspect, test, service, and replace A/C compressor clutch components or assembly.

The A/C compressor clutch assembly allows the A/C compressor to engage and disengage to modulate system pressures. The components of the compressor clutch assembly are:

- the driven plate, which is keyed to the compressor drive shaft
- the drive plate, which is integral to the drive pulley
- the clutch bearing, which operates when the clutch is disengaged
- the clutch coil, which creates the magnetic field that engages the clutch

Faulty compressor clutch bearing will make a growling noise with the engine running and the clutch disengaged. Use a digital multimeter (DMM) to test the compressor clutch by applying power and ground to the appropriate terminals and watching for clutch engagement. You must inspect the pulley and armature plate frictional surfaces for wear and oil contamination. Check the hub bearing for roughness, grease leakage, and looseness. A driven plate that drags on the drive plate or slips briefly on engagement indicates an improper clutch air gap. Adjust this air gap using shims; remove shims to decrease clearance and increase shims to increase clearance. Check the gap on any clutch service. A technician can check the clutch engagement dynamically with an ammeter in series with the clutch coil. A good clutch coil will read 2 to 4.15 amps.

Task B2.5 Inspect and correct A/C compressor lubricant level.

One must check the A/C compressor lubricant level and adjust it any time there is evidence of lubricant loss from the system. An excessive amount of oil in a refrigerant system reduces the system cooling efficiency. To check the compressor lubricant level, remove the compressor from the vehicle, drain all refrigeration oil, and refill it to manufacturer's specifications.

R-12 systems require a mineral oil with a YN-9 designation and R-134a systems with a reciprocating compressor must have a synthetic (PAG) oil designation. Rotary compressors use a different type of PAG oil. If the oils used become intermixed, compressor damage will result.

Task B2.6 Inspect, test, service, or replace A/C compressor.

You can diagnose A/C compressor internal damage using a standard A/C gauge set. Low high-side pressure and high low-side pressure on the manifold gauge set may indicate a defective compressor. A faulty compressor bearing will make a growling noise with the engine running and the compressor clutch engaged. Oil dripping from the front of the compressor indicates a faulty front seal. A rattling noise may be caused by loose compressor mounts. A growling noise that occurs when the compressor is operating is likely caused by a worn bearing in the compressor. A defective pulley will also cause a growling noise with the clutch engaged. When replacing A/C seals or O-rings, pre-lubricate them with the proper type of refrigeration oil.

Task B2.7 Inspect, repair, or replace A/C compressor mountings.

Damaged A/C compressor mounts or mounting plates can cause drive belt misalignment, improper drive belt tension, and compressor vibration. Welding can generally repair cracked mounts and mounting plates; however, care must be taken to align all parts properly.

3. Evaporator, Condenser, and Related Components (5 Questions)

Task B3.1 Inspect and correct lubricant level in evaporator, condenser, receiver/drier or accumulator/drier, and hoses when servicing or replacing components.

Most A/C system components contain refrigeration oil. When replacing the evaporator, condenser, accumulator, receiver/drier, or A/C hoses, the new component should be drained of oil, and fresh refrigeration oil should be added to manufacturer's specifications.

Task B3.2 Inspect, repair, or replace A/C system hoses, lines, filters, fittings, and seals.

You check A/C system hoses for damage and leaks during the course of any A/C system maintenance or inspection. Hoses should be replaced if they are cracked, kinked, or abraded or if the fittings show any signs of abuse. Disassemble leaking fittings and replace the O-rings. New O-rings should be lubricated with the appropriate refrigeration oil. A/C system filters and screens are used to prevent particulate (from corrosion, compressor failure, or desiccant break down) from circulating through the A/C system and must be replaced if they are clogged, restricted, or damaged. Some systems have a filter in the line between the condenser and the evaporator and some of these filters contain an orifice tube. You must install this type of filter in the proper direction.

Task B3.3 Inspect A/C condenser for proper air flow.

The A/C condenser should be checked for proper air flow at regular intervals. During a normal A/C system inspection, any bent condenser fins should be straightened and any debris should be cleaned from the condenser. Debris in the condenser air passages causes excessive high-side and low-side pressures and reduced cooling. This problem may also cause the high pressure relief valve to discharge refrigerant. Additionally, you should check the radiator shutter system for proper operation.

Task B3.4 Inspect, test, and replace A/C system condenser and mountings.

If any refrigerant tubes are kinked, cracked, or leaking, the A/C condenser must be replaced. Frost on any of the condenser tubing indicates a refrigerant passage restriction. This condition results in excessive high-side and low-side pressures and inadequate cooling. If you replace the condenser, drain the new component and install fresh refrigeration oil to manufacturer's specifications (typically 1 ounce). Condenser mounts and insulators should be checked for proper alignment and deformation which could cause abrasion and fatigue damage.

Task B3.5 Inspect and replace receiver/drier or accumulator/drier.

Most mobile A/C systems use a receiver/drier or an accumulator/drier to ensure an adequate supply of high-pressure liquid refrigerant to the system expansion. If the receiver/dryer inlet and outlet pipes have a significant temperature difference, the receiver/dryer is restricted. Frost forming on the receiver/dryer indicates an internal restriction. Bubbles and foam in the sight glass indicate rust and moisture contamination. Both of these devices contain a bag of desiccant designed to absorb and hold traces of moisture from the refrigerant. The accumulator is located at the outlet of the condenser and sometimes houses the system sight glass. The receiver is located just upstream of the system expansion device. The accumulator/drier or receiver/drier must be replaced if the A/C system has remained open to the atmosphere for an extended period of time, if there is evidence of moisture or corrosion in the system, or if catastrophic compressor failure has occurred. When the accumulator/drier or receiver/drier is replaced, the new component must be drained and fresh refrigerant oil must be added to manufacturer's specifications (typically 1 ounce).

Task B3.6 Inspect, test, and replace cab/sleeper refrigerant solenoid, expansion valve(s); adjust placement of thermal bulb (capillary tube).

One type of A/C system expansion device is the thermal expansion valve. The thermal expansion valve senses evaporator temperature using a capillary tube connected to a thermal bulb. As the fluid inside the thermal bulb expands, the orifice in the expansion valve opens to increase refrigerant flow through the evaporator. If the evaporator core temperature drops to near the freezing point, the fluid in the thermal bulb contracts and the expansion valve closes to restrict refrigerant flow. Different designs place this thermal bulb either embedded in the evaporator fins or affixed to the evaporator inlet with insulating tape.

In some systems, the expansion valve is housed in a combination valve or an "H" valve. In these systems, internal sensors monitor evaporator inlet and outlet temperatures and pressures and adjust the valve opening accordingly. A technician can diagnose a faulty expansion valve using a set of A/C pressure gauges.

Task B3.7 Inspect and replace orifice tube.

Cycling clutch-type A/C systems often use a fixed orifice tube as an expansion device. The orifice tube is located at the evaporator inlet and contains a fine screen to prevent the circulation of particulate through the evaporator core and back to the compressor. The orifice tube should be replaced if the screen is restricted or corroded, or in case of desiccant bag breakdown or catastrophic compressor failure.

A restricted orifice tube may cause lower than specified low-side pressure, frosting of the orifice tube, and inadequate cooling from the evaporator. If these conditions appear, place a shop towel soaked in hot water around the orifice tube. If the low-side pressure increases, there is moisture freezing in the orifice tube. To rectify this condition, you must recover, evacuate, and recharge the system. If the hot shop towel did not increase the low-side pressure, clean or replace the orifice tube.

Task B3.8 Inspect, test, and replace cab/sleeper evaporator.

The A/C evaporator core is located (along with the heater core and air flow control doors) in the evaporator case. One detects a leaking evaporator core most easily by measurement at the evaporator case drain, but it may also be detected at the panel and defroster vents. Also, you can remove the blower resistor assembly and go through that cavity. If the evaporator core has a leak, an oily film appears on the inside of the windshield, and the cab temperature becomes warmer than specified. If you replace an evaporator core, drain the new component and fresh refrigeration oil must be added to manufacturer's specifications (typically 3 ounces).

To find evaporator refrigerant leaks, look for oil in the leak area. A low-side pressure that is considerably lower than specified indicates evaporator restriction.

Task B3.9 Inspect, clean, and repair evaporator housing and water drain; inspect and service/replace evaporator air filter.

The evaporator case or housing contains the evaporator core, the heater core, the evaporator core drain, and the blend air and mode control doors. A clogged evaporator core drain will cause windshield fogging or a noticeable mist from the panel vents. A clogged drain can normally be opened up with a slender piece of wire or with low pressure shop air. The evaporator drain should be checked during routine maintenance inspections. A cracked evaporator case can cause a whistling noise during high blower operation. Minor cracks can be repaired using epoxy-type adhesives. A mildew smell that is noticeable during A/C system operation can be rectified by removing the evaporator case and washing it with a vinegar and water solution or a commercially available cleaner.

Task B3.10 Identify, inspect, and replace A/C system service valves (gauge connections).

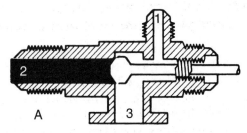

Front-Seated Position

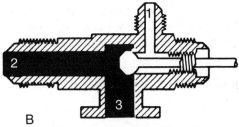

Back-Seated Position

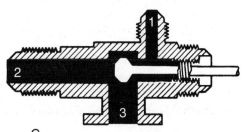

Mid-Positioned (Cracked)

   Two types of A/C system service valves are used in mobile A/C systems. Older systems use a three-position stem-type valve. Using the figure, B shows the normal operation, or back-seated position, where the valve stem is rotated counterclockwise to seat the rear valve face and seal off the service gauge port. C shows the mid-position used during A/C system diagnosis and service. A shows the front-seated position (valve stem rotated clockwise to seat the front valve face) that isolates the compressor from the A/C system. This position allows a technician to service the compressor without discharging the entire system. The system must never be operated with either service valve in the front-seated position.

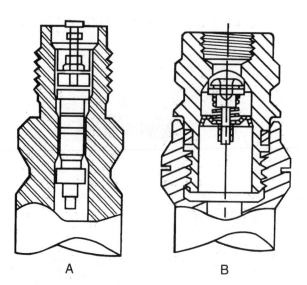

A   B

Most R-12 A/C systems use Schrader service valves. These valves resemble tire valves and may be equipped with quick connect-type fittings. R-134a systems use quick-disconnect service valves. The figure above shows both types of valves.

Task B3.11   Inspect and replace A/C system high-pressure relief device.

All mobile A/C systems are equipped with a high pressure relief device. In most systems, this device is a self-resetting relief valve, which is threaded into the high-side of the compressor. The high-pressure relief valve will vent refrigerant from the system in the event that high-side pressure exceeds safe levels.

C. Heating and Engine Cooling Systems Diagnosis, Service, and Repair (6 Questions)

Task C1   Diagnose the cause of temperature control problems in the heating/ventilation system; determine needed repairs.

System design achieves heater temperature control by one of two methods: blend air modulation or coolant flow control. In a blend air system, coolant flows through the heater core at a constant rate. Air flowing over the heater core is mixed with outside air to achieve the desired output temperature. In a coolant flow control system, temperature control is achieved by using a coolant control valve (hot-water valve) to limit the amount of coolant allowed to flow through the heater core. The coolant control valve may be vacuum or cable operated.

Task C2   Diagnose window fogging problems; determine needed repairs.

Windshield fogging may be caused by a leaking heater core or by a clogged evaporator core drain. If windshield fogging is accompanied by the smell of antifreeze, the heater core is at fault. If you smell a pungent odor, then the evaporator drain may be clogged.

Task C3   Perform engine cooling system tests for leaks, protection level, contamination, coolant level, temperature, and conditioner concentration; determine needed repairs.

To test the engine cooling system for leaks, remove the radiator pressure cap following the manufacturer's instructions. Replace the cap with a standard cooling system pressure tester and pressurize the system to operating pressure. Perform a careful visual inspection for leaks. Often you can confirm cooling system contamination with a visual inspection.

Rust in the system will turn the coolant an opaque reddish-brown color. If engine oil or transmission fluid has entered the system, the coolant will contain thick deposits resembling a milk shake. Coolant protection level is most easily determined using a cooling system hydrometer or optical sensor.

Task C4   Inspect and replace engine cooling and heating system hoses, lines, and clamps.

Cooling system and heater hoses must be replaced if they are cracked or brittle, or if they show signs of bulging or abrasion. Hose clamps should be replaced if they are deformed or cracked, or if they cannot be operated smoothly.

Task C5   Inspect, test, and replace radiator, pressure cap, and coolant recovery system (surge tank).

The technician should inspect the radiator at every scheduled (PMI) maintenance service. You check the radiator for bent fins, kinked or cracked tubes, and leaks. With the engine at normal operating temperature, the temperature of the radiator core should be uniform. Cool spots indicate clogged tubes in the core. You test the pressure cap using a cooling system pressure tester for pressure and vacuum. If the pressure cap seal, sealing gasket, or seat is damaged, the engine will overheat and coolant is lost in the recovery system. Replace the cap if it does not hold the pressure specified by the manufacturer or if there is any sign of physical damage. The coolant surge tank should be checked for leaks and for sediment build-up, and should be repaired or cleaned as necessary.

Task C6   Inspect, test, and replace water pump and drive system.

The water pump has a small weep hole directly below its drive shaft. The water pump must be replaced if there is any sign of rust or coolant leaking from the weep hole. Any lateral free play in the water pump drive shaft or a growling noise from the front of the water pump indicates a worn bearing, and warrants replacement of the water pump. Inadequate coolant conditioner level can lead to cavitation corrosion of the water pump impeller, and cause poor coolant circulation. On air clutch applications, problems in the truck air system may be the cause. If the truck's air brakes operate normally, check at the pressure protection valve.

Task C7   Inspect, test, and replace thermostats, bypasses, housing, and seals.

The only accurate way to test a thermostat is to remove it from the vehicle, place it in a container of water with a thermometer, and heat the container until the thermostat opens. The water temperature at the point when the thermostat opens should equal the manufacturer's specification for engine operating temperature. Other indications that the thermostat has opened include visible coolant flow in the upper radiator tank, a hot upper radiator hose, and an engine temperature gauge that indicates normal operating temperature.

Task C8   Flush and refill cooling system; bleed air from system.

The cooling system should be flushed if there is any sign of rust or contamination in the coolant. After flushing, the entire system should be drained and fresh coolant should be added. The technician should consult the service manual to verify cooling system capacity and bleeding procedure.

Task C9   Inspect, test, and repair or replace coolant conditioner/filter; check valves, lines, and fittings.

The coolant conditioner cartridge should be replaced during regularly scheduled maintenance services. The coolant conditioner internally lubricates cooling system components, maintains the neutrality of the coolant, filters particulate from the coolant, and prevents cavitation corrosion of the cylinder liners.

Task C10   **Inspect, test, and repair or replace fan, fan hub, fan clutch, fan controls, fan thermostat, and fan shroud.**

The technician should inspect the engine cooling fan for loose, cracked, or otherwise damaged blades. Further, inspect the fan hub for cracks. The cooling fan should be replaced, not repaired, if any damage is found. The cooling fan clutch may be a viscous-type clutch or may be operated by a thermostatic spring. Some heavy-duty trucks use a computer controlled clutch operated by either the chassis air system or engine oil hydraulic controls. The fan shroud should be inspected for cracks, and replaced as necessary. If fan blade and shroud damage is found, the technician should verify that the engine mounts are in good condition before replacing the shroud and blade.

Task C11   **Inspect, test, and replace heating system coolant control valve(s).**

The coolant control valve (hot-water valve) controls the flow of coolant through the heater core. The coolant control valve may be vacuum operated or cable operated. One can verify proper valve operation by manually opening and closing the valve and observing the temperature change in the downstream heater hose.

Task C12   **Inspect, flush, and replace heater core.**

In a poorly maintained cooling system, sediment may build up in the heater core causing poor heater performance. Flushing the heater core will restore heater efficiency and may reveal small heater core leaks. The heater core can be pressure tested independently from the rest of the cooling system; however, the core should never be pressurized in excess of normal operating pressure. When replacing a heater core, it is important to reinstall all foam mounting insulators to minimize the risk of vibration damage and to ensure a good seal around the heater core.

Task C13   **Inspect, repair, or replace radiator shutter assembly and controls.**

Many heavy-duty trucks are equipped with a radiator shutter system to facilitate engine warm-up and improve cold weather performance. Most shutter systems operate on chassis air and control occurs from the body or engine control unit. When the engine is started cold, the shutters should be fully closed. As the engine coolant temperature rises, the shutters begin to open. At normal operating temperature, the radiator shutters should be fully open.

D. Operating Systems and Related Controls Diagnosis and Repair (8 Questions)

1. Electrical (5 Questions)

Task D1.1   **Diagnose the cause of failures in HVAC electrical control systems; determine needed repairs.**

Diagnosing HVAC electrical control system problems is no different than diagnosing other electrical concerns. The technician should follow a logical approach to troubleshooting, including verifying the concern and performing a thorough visual inspection. The technician should use all available resources, including electrical schematic diagrams and service manual diagnostic routines, to locate and repair the cause of the concern.

Task D1.2 Inspect, test, and repair or replace A/C heater blower motors, resistors, switches, relays/modules, wiring, and protection devices.

A 30 amp fuse or circuit breaker generally protects the HVAC blower circuit. Many blower systems are powered by one or more relays. The operator selects the desired blower motor speed by using the blower switch. The blower resistor block contains several resistors in series, and is used to step-down the voltage to the blower motor, thereby providing multiple blower speeds. The resistor block usually contains a thermal fuse to prevent blower motor damage in case of a high current draw.

Task D1.3 Inspect, test, and repair or replace A/C compressor clutch relays/modules, wiring, sensors, switches, diodes, and protection devices.

The A/C compressor clutch coil is generally powered by an electronically controlled relay. The compressor clutch relay may be controlled by the body control unit or by the engine control unit. Many blower motor circuits connect the motor switch and resistor strings to the ground side of the motor. When the system is on, positive current flows to one brush in the motor, then to the other brush and on to ground through the resistor assembly. When you set the blower to high, the motor brush grounds directly through the motor switch contacts at the high speed relay. If you select one of the lower speeds, the brush grounds through that specific blower resistor.

Task D1.4 Inspect, test, repair or replace, and adjust A/C-related engine control systems.

A/C compressor clutch operation may be dependent upon signals from various engine sensors. Faulty engine-related components that affect A/C system operation can usually be diagnosed using a hand-held scan tool or a laptop PC interface. The engine control unit or body control unit will disable the A/C compressor clutch if the engine coolant temperature is too high or if the outside air temperature is too low. On vehicles with an electronically controlled automatic transmission, the compressor clutch can be disengaged briefly during shifts. The radiator shutter system is disabled (shutters are fully open) during A/C system operation.

Task D1.5 Inspect, test, repair, and replace engine cooling/condenser fan motors, relays/modules, switches, sensors, wiring, and protection devices.

Some trucks are equipped with electric engine cooling fans and electric condenser fans. Electric fans are usually controlled by an electronic relay which is in turn controlled by the engine control unit or the body control unit of the engine fuel system computer. The engine computer grounds the low and high speed fan relays in response to engine coolant temperature and compressor head temperature. When the engine coolant temperature reaches 212°F (100°C), the engine computer grounds the low-speed fan relay. If the coolant temperature reaches 226°F (108°C), the computer grounds the high speed relay.

Task D1.6 Inspect, test, adjust, repair, and replace electric actuator motors, relays/modules, switches, sensors, wiring, and protection devices.

Some HVAC systems control blend air and mode doors with electronic actuators. Electronic actuators contain a small motor, a gear train, and feedback device to indicate the position of the controlled door to the controlling processor. Some electronic systems contain self-diagnostic abilities with diagnostic trouble codes (DTC). You typically diagnose these with a scan tool or laptop computer. On some systems, you can adjust the actuator doors.

Task D1.7 Inspect, test, service, or replace HVAC system electrical control panel assemblies.

Electrical control panel assemblies for manual and semi-automatic HVAC systems are modular in design, allowing for replacement of individual switches and illumination bulbs without replacing the entire panel. Most electronic ATC control panels allow the technician access only to replace illumination bulbs.

2. Air/Vacuum/Mechanical (2 Questions)

Task D2.1 Diagnose the cause of failures in HVAC air, vacuum, mechanical switches and controls; determine needed repairs.

The most common cause of failures in HVAC air and vacuum systems is leaking hoses and diaphragms. Air and vacuum leaks can often be located by listening for a hissing noise. To locate minor air leaks, brush a mild soap solution over fittings and connections and watch for bubbles. To check for vacuum leaks, use a hand-held vacuum pump (Mitivac) to supply 20 in. Hg. to one end of the vacuum hose while the other end is plugged or attached to its device. The hose should hold 15 to 20 in. Hg., without leaking.

Task D2.2 Inspect, test, service, or replace HVAC system air/vacuum/mechanical control panel assemblies.

HVAC vacuum and mechanical control panel assemblies require very little testing and maintenance. A leaking vacuum switch will hiss in one or more positions. Broken control cable arms or anchors will result in ineffective control levers.

Task D2.3 Inspect, test, adjust, or replace HVAC system air/vacuum/mechanical control cables and linkages.

A technician replaces HVAC control cables if they are kinked or seized due to internal corrosion. One must adjust control cables to allow a full range of motion for the control lever and for the output device.

Task D2.4 Inspect, test, and replace HVAC system vacuum actuators (diaphragms/motors) and hoses.

You can evaluate the performance of vacuum actuators and hoses by using a hand-held vacuum pump. Vacuum systems are tested by applying vacuum to the upstream (input) end of the system while individual components must be tested at the component connection. Connect the vacuum pump to each vacuum actuator and supply 15 to 20 in. Hg. to the actuator. Check the vacuum actuator rod to be sure it moves freely. Close the vacuum pump valve and observe the vacuum gauge. The gauge reading should remain steady for at least 1 minute. If the gauge reading drops slowly, the actuator is leaking. You replace any hoses or components that do not hold vacuum or do not operate properly.

Task D2.5 Identify, inspect, test, and replace HVAC system vacuum reservoir(s), check valve(s), and restrictors.

In HVAC systems that use vacuum switches and actuators, a vacuum reservoir and check valve are installed between the vacuum source and the control panel. The check valve is a one-way valve that allows the reservoir to hold constant vacuum regardless of fluctuations in the vacuum source. The vacuum reservoir supplies vacuum at a consistent level during periods of low-source vacuum (during long uphill runs or engine lugging). The check valve must be replaced if it leaks or if it passes vacuum in both directions. The reservoir must be replaced if it will not hold vacuum. When vacuum is supplied with vacuum pump to the reservoir, it should hold 15 to 20 in. Hg.

Task D2.6 Identify, inspect, test, and replace air pressure regulator valve, lines, and hoses.

A compressor governor or an internal unloader assembly generally regulates the pressure in the chassis air system. If a governor or unloader fails, a pressure relief valve will release air from the system to prevent damage to system components. The pressure relief valve will operate at about 150 psi. Before replacing any chassis air system component, the system must be drained of air pressure.

Task D2.7 Inspect, test, adjust, repair, or replace HVAC system ducts, doors, and outlets.

Misaligned or improperly installed HVAC ducts will cause reduced levels of system output air. Blend air and mode control doors must be adjusted to allow a full range of motion when controls are operated.

3. Automatic Temperature Control (ATC) (1 Question)

Task D3.1 Diagnose automatic temperature control system problems; determine needed repairs.

Most ATC systems provide internal diagnostic capabilities. On some ATC systems, diagnostic trouble codes may be displayed digitally on the control panel while on other systems a hand-held scan tool or PC interface must be used to retrieve codes. The technician should always refer to diagnostic routines in the vehicle service manual when attempting to troubleshoot ATC codes. Most importantly, the technician must rule out the possibility of mechanical failures before searching for electronic malfunctions.

Task D3.2 Inspect, test, adjust, or replace climate control temperature sensors.

ATC systems rely on a variety of sensors to provide feedback to the ATC control unit. The control unit uses the sensor signals to determine how much heating or cooling is required to maintain the desired cab or sleeper temperature. The ambient temperature sensor monitors outside air temperature. The engine coolant temperature sensor monitors engine coolant temperature. The ATC temperature (or interior temperature) sensor monitors the temperature of the air in the cab or the sleeper box. Some ATC sensors are connected to the temperature selector lever with an adjustable cable. A sunlight sensor is used on some vehicles to monitor the intensity of the light coming through the windshield.

Task D3.3 Inspect, test, adjust, and replace temperature blend door/power servo system.

Most ATC systems achieve temperature modulation by blending air that has passed through the A/C evaporator core with air that has passed through the heater core. The volume of air that is allowed to pass through each core is regulated by a blend air door. The blend air door is controlled by the blend door actuator, which consists of an electric motor, a gear train, and a feedback device. The feedback device provides precise information about the position of the blend air door to the control unit. The blend door actuator must be replaced if the drive gears are worn or damaged, if the motor develops a dead spot or if the feedback device fails. A faulty feedback device will cause the motor to either "hunt" for the desired position or to be inoperative.

Task D3.4 Inspect, test, adjust, and replace heater water valve and controls.

Some ATC systems use a coolant control valve to regulate the flow of coolant through the heater core. The coolant control valve on ATC systems is usually vacuum controlled and is not adjustable. A faulty coolant control valve can generally be diagnosed visually.

Task D3.5 Inspect, test, adjust, and replace electric, air, and vacuum motors, solenoids, and switches.

In most ATC systems, the mode doors are controlled using electronic actuators that are similar to the blend door actuator. Faulty mode door actuators are usually diagnosed by following diagnostic routines in the vehicle service manual.

Task D3.6 Inspect, test, and replace ATC control panel.

The only serviceable components in most ATC control panels are illumination bulbs. Faulty ATC control panels are generally diagnosed by following diagnostic routines in the vehicle service manual.

Task D3.7 Inspect, test, adjust, or replace ATC microprocessor (climate control computer/programmer).

The ATC control unit may be integral to the control panel or it may be a 'stand-alone' component. In either event, the control unit is generally multiplexed to the engine and/or body control units, thereby providing electronic diagnostic capabilities in case of control unit failure.

Task D3.8 Check and adjust calibration of ATC system.

The easiest way to check the calibration of the ATC system is to use a small thermometer to monitor the interior temperature of the cab and sleeper and to compare the actual temperature to the temperature setting on the control panel. In systems that use a cable-operated ATC sensor, the cable can be adjusted to accommodate small deviations from the set temperature. In most other applications, deviations from the set temperature are usually caused by a faulty sensor.

E. Refrigerant Recovery, Recycling, and Handling (4 Questions)

NOTE: Tasks 1 through 5 should be accomplished in accordance with published EPA and appropriate SAE "J" standards for R-12, R-134a, and approved refrigerant blends.

Task E1   Maintain and verify correct operation of certified equipment.

The Clean Air Act (CAA) establishes the following rules for record keeping and operation of certified refrigeration service equipment:

1. "Any person who owns approved refrigerant recycling equipment certified under the act must maintain records of the name and address of any facility to which refrigerant is sent."
2. "Any person who owns approved refrigerant recycling equipment must retain records demonstrating that all persons authorized to operate the equipment are certified under the act."
3. "Public Notification: Any person who conducts any retail sales of a Class I or Class II substance must prominently display a sign that reads: 'It is a violation of federal law to sell containers of Class I and Class II refrigerant of less than 20 pounds of such refrigerant to any one who is not properly trained and certified.'"

4. "Any person who sells or distributes any Class I or Class II substance that is in a container of less than 20 pounds of such refrigerant must verify that the purchaser is certified, and must retain records for a period of three years." These records must be maintained on-site.

Task E2   Identify and recover A/C system refrigerant.

According to Department of Transportation (DOT)/Air Conditioning and Refrigeration Institute (ARI) guidelines, 4B4 cylinders used to store recovered refrigerant shall ultimately be painted gray with the top shoulder portion painted yellow. The refrigerant type to be stored in a given container must be clearly marked on the container's label. For recovery/recycling purposes, only cylinders that are identified for recovered refrigerant may be used. Never use a cylinder that is intended to contain new refrigerant to store recovered refrigerant. Returnable/reusable cylinders meet DOT specification 4BA-300. These cylinders are characterized by a combined liquid/vapor valve, located at the top.

Task E3   Recycle refrigerant.

Differences between the terms recover, recycle, and reclaim must be completely understood and properly used within the industry. To recover refrigerant is to remove refrigerant in any condition from a system and store it in an external container. The refrigerant must then either be recycled on-site or shipped off-site for reclamation. To recycle refrigerant is to reduce contaminants in used refrigerant by oil separation with single or multiple passes through devices such as replaceable filter driers, which reduce moisture, acidity, and particulate matter. To reclaim refrigerant is to reprocess refrigerant to new product specifications by means which may include distillation. Chemical analysis of the refrigerant is required to assure that appropriate product specifications are met. Reclamation usually implies the use of procedures available only at processing or manufacturing facilities.

Task E4   Handle, label, and store refrigerant.

Any portable container used for transfer of reclaimed or recycled refrigerant must conform to DOT and United Laboratories (UL) standards. Before introducing refrigerant into an approved storage cylinder, the cylinder must be evacuated to at least 27 inches of mercury. Cylinder-safe filling level must be monitored by measured weight. Shut-off valves are required within 12 inches (30 cm) of service hose ends. Shut-off valves must remain closed while connecting and disconnecting hoses to vehicle air conditioning service ports. Safety goggles should always be worn while working with or around refrigerant.

Task E5   Test recycled refrigerant for non-condensable gases.

To test a refrigerant for non-condensable gases, compare the pressure of the refrigerant in a cylinder to the theoretical pressure of pure refrigerant at a given temperature. If the actual pressure in the cylinder is lower than the theoretical pressure, the refrigerant is contaminated with non-condensable gas.

 **Sample Test for Practice**

Sample Test

Please note the letter and number in parentheses following each question. They match the overview in section 4 that discusses the relevant subject matter. You may want to refer to the overview using this cross-referencing key to help with questions posing problems for you.

1. There is a growling or rumbling noise at the A/C compressor. When the clutch engages the noise stops. Technician A says the compressor bearing is defective. Technician B says the clutch bearing is defective. Who is right?
   A. Technician A only
   B. Technician B only
   C. Both A and B
   D. Neither A nor B
   (A1)

2. A strange odor comes from the panel vents while operating the A/C in NORMAL mode. Technician A says he can smell R-12 anywhere: the truck must have a leaking evaporator. Technician B says the heater core must be leaking. Who is right?
   A. Technician A only
   B. Technician B only
   C. Both A and B
   D. Neither A nor B
   (A2)

3. An HVAC system outputs air at a constant temperature, regardless of the temperature setting. The most likely cause is:
   A. a low refrigerant charge.
   B. low coolant level.
   C. a compressor clutch failure.
   D. a broken blend door cable.
   (A3)

4. Before a portable container is used to transfer recycled R-12, it must be evacuated to at least:
   A. 20 in. Hg.
   B. 22 in. Hg.
   C. 27 in. Hg.
   D. 12 in. Hg.
   (E4)

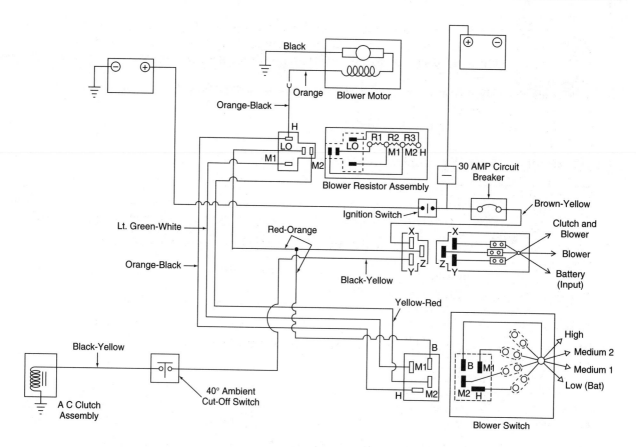

5. Refer to the figure shown above. When the blower switch is in the medium-2 position, how many resistors are used in the circuit to control blower motor speed?
   A. Three
   B. Two
   C. One
   D. None

(D1.2)

6. Refer to the same figure used in question 5. All of the following could prevent the A/C clutch from engaging **EXCEPT:**
   A. a faulty 30 amp circuit breaker.
   B. ambient temperature below 40 degrees.
   C. the ambient temperature cutout switch stuck closed.
   D. open circuit in the black-yellow wire.

(D1.1)

7. Which is the best method of removing particulate from an A/C system after a mechanical failure?
   A. Solvent flushing
   B. R-11 flushing
   C. In-line filter
   D. Nitrogen flushing

(B1.7)

8. To avoid mixing refrigerants, SAE J2197 standard specifies that R-134a service hose fittings for connection to manifold gauge sets or to recovery/recycling/charging equipment are to be:
   A. 3/16 inch, 16 ACME thread.
   B. 3/16 inch, 14 ACME thread.
   C. 1/2 inch, 16 ACME thread.
   D. 1/4 inch, 16 ACME thread.

(E2)

9. A heater does not supply the cab with enough heat. The coolant level and blower are OK. Technician A says an improperly adjusted temperature control cable could be the cause. Technician B says a clogged heater core could be the cause. Who is right?
   A. Technician A only
   B. Technician B only
   C. Both A and B
   D. Neither A nor B   (C1)

10. The low pressure cut-out switch senses pressure in the:
    A. system high side.
    B. atmosphere.
    C. system low side.
    D. cab/sleeper.   (B2.2)

11. When evacuating an A/C system, which manifold gauge hose is connected to the vacuum pump?
    A. The high pressure hose
    B. The low pressure hose
    C. The center service hose
    D. Any hose   (B1.6)

12. The cab temperature sensor in an ATC system operates under the same electrical principal as a(n):
    A. intake air temperature sensor.
    B. heated oxygen sensor.
    C. hot wire air flow meter.
    D. throttle position sensor.   (D3.2)

13. Owners of approved refrigerant recycling equipment must maintain records that demonstrate:
    A. only certified technicians operate equipment.
    B. equipment is operated under the supervision of certified technicians.
    C. technicians who are undergoing certification training operate equipment.
    D. equipment is operated only when a certified technician is on the premises. (E1)

14. The process that reduces contaminants in used refrigerant by using oil separation and filter core driers is:
    A. restoration.
    B. recovery.
    C. recycling.
    D. reclamation.   (E3)

15. Technician A says that the ATC control panel can be reprogrammed using a hand-held scan tool. Technician B says that a hand-held scan tool can be used to help diagnose ATC system failures. Who is right?
    A. Technician A only
    B. Technician B only
    C. Both A and B
    D. Neither A nor B   (D3.7)

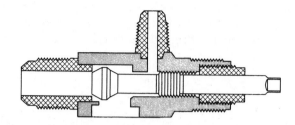

16. What is the position of the service valve shown in the figure above?
    A. Front-seated position
    B. Back-seated position
    C. Mid-position
    D. Normal operating position   (B2.6)

17. Technician A says bubbles and or foam in the sight glass indicate the refrigerant charge is low and air has entered the system. Technician B says a cloudy sight glass indicates moisture in the system. Who is right?
    A. Technician A only
    B. Technician B only
    C. Both A and B
    D. Neither A nor B   (B1.3)

18. All of the following can cause A/C compressor drive belt misalignment **EXCEPT**:
    A. a bent compressor mounting bracket holder.
    B. a faulty compressor clutch bearing assembly.
    C. an improperly set compressor clutch air gap.
    D. a faulty idler pulley.   (B1.2)

Pressure-Temperature Relationship

Temperature °F(°C)	R-12 PSIG (bar/kg/cm²)	R-134A PSIG (bar/kg/cm²)
–15 (–26.1)	2.5 (.17/.18)	0 (0)
–10 (–23.3)	4.5 (.31/.32)	2.0 (.14/.14)
–5 (–20.5)	6.7 (.46/.03)	4.1 (.28/.29)
0 (–17.8)	9.2 (.63/.65)	6.5 (.45/.46)
5 (–15.0)	11.8 (.81/.83)	9.1 (.63/.64)
10 (–12.2)	14.7 (1.0/1.0)	12.0 (.89/.84)
15 (–9.4)	17.7 (1.2/1.2)	15.1 (1.0/1.2)
20 (–6.7)	21.1 (1.5/1.5)	18.4 (1.3/1.3)
25 (–3.9)	24.6 (1.7/1.7)	22.1 (1.5/1.6)
30 (–1.1)	28.5 (2.0./2.0)	26.1 (1.8/1.8)
35 (1.7)	32.6 (2.2/2.3)	30.4 (2.1/2.1)
40 (4.4)	37.0 (2.6/2.6)	35.0 (2.4/2.5)
45 (7.2)	41.7 (2.9/3.0)	40.0 (2.8/2.8)
50 (10.0)	46.7 (3.2/3.3)	45.4 (3.1/3.2)
55 (12.8)	52.1 (3.6/3.7)	51.2 (3.5/3.6)
60 (15.6)	57.8 (4.0/4.1)	57.4 (4.0/4.0)
65 (18.3)	63.8 (4.4/4.5)	64.0 (4.4/4.5)
70 (21.1)	70.2 (4.8/5.0)	71.1 (5.0/5.0)
75 (23.9)	77.0 (5.3/5.4)	78.6 (5.4/5.5)
80 (26.7)	84.2 (5.8/6.0)	86.7 (6.0/6.1)
85 (29.4)	91.7 (6.3/6.4)	95.2 (6.6/6.7)
90 (32.2)	99.7(6.9/7.0)	104.3 (7.2/7.3)
95 (35.0)	108.2 (7.5/7.6)	113.9 (7.9/8.0)
100 (37.8)	117.0 (8.1/8.2)	124.1 (8.6/8.7)
105 (40.6)	126.4 (8.7/8.9)	134.9 (9.3/9.5)
110 (43.3)	136.2 (9.4/9.6)	146.3 (10.1/10.3)
115 (46.1)	146.5 (10.1/10.3)	158.4 (11.0/11.1)
120 (48.9)	157.3 (11.0/11.1)	171.1 (11.8/12.0)

19. A storage container or air conditioning system containing R-12 (at rest and subject to an ambient temperature of 70°F will have an internal gauge pressure of approximately (see table shown on previous page):
   A. 220 psi.
   B. 125 psi.
   C. 70 psi.
   D. 30 psi.   (B1.3)

20. What will the halide leak detector flame color be when the search hose is placed near a large refrigerant leak?
   A. Red
   B. Yellow-green
   C. Pale blue
   D. Purple   (B1.5)

21. Technician A says that the heater control valve can be operated by engine speed. Technician B says that the heater control valve can be cable-operated. Who is right?
   A. Technician A only
   B. Technician B only
   C. Both A and B
   D. Neither A nor B   (D2.3)

22. While testing a heater core for leaks, you apply 10 psi of air pressure. The pressure bleeds to 5 psi in 3 minutes. You should conclude that:
   A. the core is OK.
   B. the core may require repair in future.
   C. the core leaks and needs repair now.
   D. this is not a valid test for a leaking heater core.   (C12)

23. An A/C compressor has a stripped mounting bolthole. Technician A says the threads can be restored by applying a weld to the damaged area and then drilling and retapping the hole. Technician B says the compressor must be replaced, not repaired. Who is right?
   A. Technician A only
   B. Technician B only
   C. Both A and B
   D. Neither A nor B   (B2.7)

24. Raising the pressure in the cooling system:
   A. lowers the boiling point of the coolant.
   B. raises the boiling point of the coolant.
   C. prevents corrosion in the cooling system.
   D. does not affect the boiling point of the coolant.   (C5)

25. In servicing the expansion valve, which of the following can a technician perform:
   A. adjust the expansion valve using a torque wrench.
   B. adjust the expansion valve using an Allen wrench.
   C. adjust the expansion valve using a screwdriver.
   D. the expansion valve cannot be adjusted.   (B3.6)

26. Technician A says that according to new environmental laws, shut-off valves must be located no more than 20 inches from test hose service ends. Technician B says that according to new environmental laws, shut-off valves must be located no more than 12 inches from test hose service ends. Who is right?
   A. Technician A only
   B. Technician B only
   C. Both A and B
   D. Neither A nor B   (E5)

27. The lubricant used in R-134a mobile A/C systems is:
    A. a polyalkylene glycol (PAG) based lubricant.
    B. a mineral based petroleum lubricant.
    C. DEXRON or DEXRON II lubricant.
    D. type C-3 SAE 30 based oil lubricant.   (B1.9)

28. A customer complains that he is unable to control the output temperature of his
    HVAC system. The most likely cause of this problem is:
    A. a broken blend door cable.
    B. a defective compressor clutch.
    C. a clogged orifice tube.
    D. a defective blower switch.   (B1.1)

29. ATC systems may use any of the following sensors **EXCEPT:**
    A. a sun sensor.
    B. an ambient temperature sensor.
    C. an evaporator temperature sensor.
    D. a manifold pressure sensor.   (D3.2)

30. During normal A/C operation a loud hissing noise is heard and a cloud of vapor
    rolls from under the vehicle. Technician A says that the excessive high-side
    pressure that caused the pressure relief valve on the A/C compressor to operate
    might have been the result of a faulty engine cooling fan clutch. Technician B says
    that the relief valve might have operated due to a faulty shutter control solenoid.
    Who is right?
    A. Technician A only
    B. Technician B only
    C. Both A and B
    D. Neither A nor B   (B2.1)

31. During a performance test, the technician notices that the A/C compressor clutch
    is slipping. Technician A says that the air gap was probably set improperly.
    Technician B says that the pressure plate needs to be resurfaced. Who is right?
    A. Technician A only
    B. Technician B only
    C. Both A and B
    D. Neither A nor B   (B2.4)

32. To check and adjust the A/C compressor lubricant level:
    A. quickly purge the system and add oil charges to refill it.
    B. open the drain plug and crank the engine until the compressor is empty, then
       pump fresh oil into the compressor.
    C. remove the compressor from the vehicle, drain the oil, and add the specified
       quantity of fresh oil.
    D. add refrigerant oil until you can see the oil level.   (B2.5)

33. Refrigerant oil must be added to the new component prior to installation when
    replacing any of the following **EXCEPT:**
    A. the evaporator.
    B. the condenser.
    C. the accumulator.
    D. the suction throttling valve.   (B3.1)

34. Air flow through the A/C condenser will be significantly affected by all of the
    following **EXCEPT:**
    A. debris trapped in the fins.
    B. relative humidity of the outside air.
    C. bent cooling fins.
    D. vehicle speed.   (B3.3)

35. Technician A says that deformed or improperly aligned condenser mounting insulators will not damage the A/C system. Technician B says that deformed or improperly aligned condenser mounting insulators could damage the condenser and refrigerant lines. Who is right?
    A. Technician A only
    B. Technician B only
    C. Both A and B
    D. Neither A nor B   (B3.4)

36. The receiver/drier must be replaced:
    A. if the A/C system has been open to the atmosphere for an extended period of time.
    B. when the A/C system is evacuated and charged.
    C. every 100,000 miles.
    D. if the compressor is replaced.   (B3.5)

37. When attempting to verify a leaking evaporator core, the technician is LEAST likely to sense refrigerant with the detector probe:
    A. at the evaporator case drain.
    B. over the expansion valve.
    C. at the panel vents.
    D. at the defroster vents.   (B3.8)

38. To eliminate a mildew smell from the A/C output air:
    A. remove the evaporator case, clean it with a vinegar and water solution, and dry it thoroughly before reinstallation.
    B. spray a disinfectant into the panel outlets.
    C. pour a small amount of alcohol into the air intake plenum.
    D. place an automotive deodorizer under the dash.   (B3.9)

39. Technician A says the Schrader service valve has a removable core. Technician B says the Schrader service valve must be rear seated during A/C compressor operation. Who is right?
    A. Technician A only
    B. Technician B only
    C. Both A and B
    D. Neither A nor B   (B3.10)

40. The A/C high-pressure relief valve shows evidence of slight oil leakage. Technician A says you must replace the valve and repair the leak. Technician B says that if the valve is just leaking a little oil and not refrigerant, replacement is not necessary. Who is right?
    A. Technician A only
    B. Technician B only
    C. Both A and B
    D. Neither A nor B   (B3.11)

41. With the HVAC system in the DEFROST mode, the blower on HIGH, and the temperature control on COLD, the bottom of the windshield fogs up on the outside because:
    A. the evaporator drain is clogged.
    B. the heater core leaks.
    C. the evaporator core is iced up.
    D. the cold windshield causes moisture to condense from the outside air. (C2)

42. The tool most commonly used to determine the protection level of engine coolant is:
    A. a hydrometer.
    B. a spectrophotometer.
    C. a balance scale.
    D. a color gauge.   (C3)

43. The upper radiator hose has a slight bulge. Technician A says that the hose does not need to be replaced unless it appears cracked. Technician B says that the bulge indicates a weak spot and the hose should be replaced. Who is right?
    A. Technician A only
    B. Technician B only
    C. Both A and B
    D. Neither A nor B   (C4)

44. A growling noise is coming from the water pump. Technician A says that the water pump bearing is the cause. Technician B says that the stator has been eroded by cavitation. Who is right?
    A. Technician A only
    B. Technician B only
    C. Both A and B
    D. Neither A nor B   (C6)

45. All of the following are good methods of verifying that the thermostat opens **EXCEPT:**
    A. feeling the upper radiator hose.
    B. watching the temperature gauge.
    C. watching for motion in the upper radiator tank.
    D. watching the surge tank.   (C7)

46. All of these statements about cooling system service are true **EXCEPT:**
    A. when the cooling system pressure is increased, the boiling point is decreased.
    B. if more antifreeze is added to the coolant mix, the boiling point is increased.
    C. a good quality ethylene glycol antifreeze contains a corrosion inhibitor.
    D. coolant solutions must be recovered, recycled, or handled as hazardous material.   (C8)

47. Technician A says that you should replace the coolant conditioner cartridge at regular maintenance intervals. Technician B says that the coolant conditioner cartridge only helps to break in the engine and does not need to be replaced. Who is right?
    A. Technician A only
    B. Technician B only
    C. Both A and B
    D. Neither A nor B   (C9)

48. Technician A says that a cracked fan blade should be welded. Technician B says that a cracked fan blade can be repaired with epoxy. Who is right?
    A. Technician A only
    B. Technician B only
    C. Both A and B
    D. Neither A nor B   (C10)

49. When replacing the coolant control valve:
    A. the technician must drain the entire cooling system.
    B. the technician does not need to drain the entire cooling system.
    C. the technician must replace the control cable.
    D. there is no need to bleed the system.   (C11)

50. If the radiator shutter assembly does not close:
    A. the engine will overheat.
    B. high-side pressure will be excessive.
    C. the air pressure relief valve cannot operate.
    D. the engine will take longer to warm up.   (C13)

51. Technician A says that the binary pressure switch prevents compressor operation if the refrigerant charge has been lost or ambient temperature too cold. Technician B says that the binary pressure switch turns off the compressor if the system pressure is too high. Who is right?
    A. Technician A only
    B. Technician B only
    C. Both A and B
    D. Neither A nor B   (D1.3)

52. A signal to the power train control module from which of the following sensors could cause the A/C compressor to disengage?
    A. Engine coolant temperature (ECT) sensor
    B. Intake air temperature (IAT) sensor
    C. Heated oxygen sensor (HO2S)
    D. Cooling fan control sensor   (D1.4)

53. An electric cooling fan motor can be controlled by any of the following **EXCEPT:**
    A. an electronic relay.
    B. an independent electronic module.
    C. a multiplexed electronic module.
    D. an air solenoid controller.   (D1.5)

54. The blend door actuator motor is generally mounted:
    A. using epoxy.
    B. using butylene sealer.
    C. behind the glove box.
    D. to the evaporator case.   (D1.6)

55. Technician A says that if there is no output from the blower motor switch, you replace the switch. Technician B says that feedback from the blower motor resistors could be the cause. Who is right?
    A. Technician A only
    B. Technician B only
    C. Both A and B
    D. Neither A nor B   (D2.1)

56. Technician A says that epoxy should be used to repair a broken temperature control lever. Technician B says that a temperature control head with a broken lever should be replaced. Who is right?
    A. Technician A only
    B. Technician B only
    C. Both A and B
    D. Neither A nor B   (D2.2)

57. The proper method of testing a vacuum actuator is to:
    A. apply shop air to the vacuum port and listen for leaks.
    B. use a hand-held vacuum pump and observe the gauge.
    C. move the control lever and verify that the actuator plunger moves.
    D. apply vacuum using an A/C evacuation pump and verify that the actuator plunger moves.   (D2.4)

58. What purpose does a vacuum check valve have in an HVAC system?
    A. To monitor vacuum in all HVAC systems.
    B. To delay vacuum to the actuators until the coolant has reached operating temperature.
    C. To prevent shock damage to vacuum actuator diaphragms.
    D. To prevent loss of vacuum to components during periods of low engine vacuum.   (D2.5)

59. All of the following statements about the chassis air system are true **EXCEPT:**
    A. it is important to keep water drained from the system.
    B. air from the system can be used to operate the fan clutch.
    C. air from the system can be used to operate the radiator shutters.
    D. the chassis air system is integral with the air-operated fan clutch.   (D2.6)

60. A whistling noise coming from under the dash while the HVAC system is being operated with the blower on HIGH could indicate:
    A. a misaligned duct.
    B. a defective vacuum actuator.
    C. an improperly adjusted mode door cable.
    D. a poor electrical connection to the blend door motor.   (D2.7)

61. On a vehicle equipped with ATC, the blend door actuator motor runs when the temperature setting is changed, but the blend door does not move. The most likely cause of this problem is:
    A. a defective control module.
    B. a defective actuator feedback device.
    C. a defective drive gear in the actuator.
    D. an improperly adjusted ATC sensor cable.   (D3.3)

62. Automatic temperature control systems may use a coolant control valve that is operated using any of the following **EXCEPT:**
    A. chassis air pressure.
    B. vacuum.
    C. a cable.
    D. a magneto.   (D3.4)

63. The most useful tool for diagnosing electric actuators and solenoids in an ATC system is:
    A. a 12-volt test light.
    B. a self-powered test light.
    C. a hand-held scan tool.
    D. an A/C system charging station.   (D3.5)

64. One segment of the digital readout on an ATC control panel is inoperative. Technician A says that the control panel should be replaced. Technician B says that the Light Emitting Diode (LED) can be replaced. Who is right?
    A. Technician A only
    B. Technician B only
    C. Both A and B
    D. Neither A nor B   (D3.6)

65. Technician A says you check the calibration of an ATC system using A/C gauges only. Technician B says you can recalibrate all ATC systems in the field. Who is right?
    A. Technician A only
    B. Technician B only
    C. Both A and B
    D. Neither A nor B   (D3.8)

66. All of the following statements about charging an A/C system are true **EXCEPT:**
    A. Refrigerant may be installed through both service valves when the engine is not running.
    B. Refrigerant may be installed through the low-side service valve when the engine is running.
    C. Refrigerant may be installed through both service ports when the engine is running.
    D. You may install refrigerant directly from an approved charging station.   (B1.8)

67. A band of frost on the A/C high pressure hose, upstream from the orifice tube
    indicates:
    A. a faulty compressor discharge valve.
    B. a restriction in the high pressure hose.
    C. a clogged orifice tube.
    D. moisture in the system.   (B1.4)

68. The STV, POA, ETR, and EPR valves:
    A. control evaporator pressure.
    B. control condenser pressure.
    C. control compressor pressure.
    D. control liquid line pressure.   (B3.7)

69. Which of the following can be used to lubricate replacement A/C hose O-rings?
    A. Petroleum jelly
    B. Transmission fluid
    C. Silicone grease
    D. Refrigeration oil   (B3.2)

70. Technician A says the HVAC control panel sometimes contains replaceable
    components. Technician B says that you have to replace the HVAC control panel
    as a unit, if any of the components fail. Who is right?
    A. Technician A only
    B. Technician B only
    C. Both A and B
    D. Neither A nor B   (D1.7)

71. An ATC system controls all of the following **EXCEPT:**
    A. the engine cooling fan.
    B. the blower motor speed.
    C. the blend door actuator.
    D. the outside air door position.   (D3.1)

6 Additional Test Questions for Practice

Additional Test Questions

Please note the letter and number in parentheses following each question. They match the overview in section 4 that discusses the relevant subject matter. You may want to refer to the overview using this cross-referencing key to help with questions posing problems for you.

1. Technician A says that a clogged heater core could cause insufficient heater output. Technician B says that an improperly adjusted coolant control valve cable could cause insufficient heater output. Who is right?
   A. Technician A only
   B. Technician B only
   C. Both A and B
   D. Neither A nor B   (C1)

2. Poor cooling from the A/C system that uses a STV valve can be caused by all of the following **EXCEPT:**
   A. the fan clutch always engaged.
   B. an improperly adjusted blend door cable.
   C. a low refrigerant charge.
   D. a refrigerant overcharge.   (B1.1)

3. Never operate the compressor with the high-side service valve:
   A. back-seated.
   B. front-seated.
   C. in mid-position.
   D. hot.   (B3.10)

4. The water pump should be replaced any time:
   A. the fan clutch is replaced.
   B. the heater hoses are replaced.
   C. there is a small leak from the weep hole.
   D. the thermostat sticks closed.   (C6)

5. What is the source of most non-condensable gases in refrigerant?
   A. Acid
   B. Air
   C. Moisture
   D. Oil   (E5)

6. When replacing a thermostat, the side with the spring:
   A. must be installed facing the housing.
   B. must be installed facing forward.
   C. must be installed facing the heater core.
   D. must be installed facing the engine block.   (C7)

7. The thermal bulb and capillary tube:
   A. are fastened to the condenser fins using epoxy.
   B. are located in the accumulator.
   C. are kept in contact with the evaporator inlet using insulating tape.
   D. are an integral part of the fixed orifice.   (B3.6)

8. Technician A says that you should replace the receiver/drier if the sight glass appears cloudy. Technician B says that you should only replace the receiver/drier if it has a leak. Who is right?
   A. Technician A only
   B. Technician B only
   C. Both A and B
   D. Neither A nor B   (B3.5)

9. Which of the following is LEAST likely to cause windshield fogging in the DEFROST mode?
   A. A leaking heater core
   B. A clogged evaporator drain
   C. An exterior water leak into the plenum chamber
   D. Moisture in the refrigerant   (C2)

10. A whistling noise coming from under the passenger side dash with the blower motor on high speed might indicate:
    A. a clogged evaporator drain.
    B. a cracked evaporator case.
    C. a broken blend door cable.
    D. a low refrigerant charge.   (B3.9)

11. Technician A says that the best way to ensure that an A/C compressor has the proper amount of lubricant is to drain the compressor and add lubricant to the manufacturer's specifications. Technician B says if you have a doubt about the lubricant level just add an oil charge to the system. Who is right?
    A. Technician A only
    B. Technician B only
    C. Both A and B
    D. Neither A nor B   (B2.5)

12. Coolant conditioner performs all of the following tasks **EXCEPT:**
    A. raises the boiling point of the coolant.
    B. filters rust and debris from the coolant.
    C. lubricates the cooling system internally.
    D. prevents cavitation corrosion of the cylinder liners.   (C9)

13. The A/C compressor drive belt should be adjusted:
    A. using a belt tension gauge.
    B. so there is no deflection at maximum engine speed.
    C. so there is no static deflection.
    D. as tightly as possible.   (B2.3)

14. During an HVAC performance test, the technician notices that the A/C compressor outlet is nearly as hot as the upper radiator hose. Technician A says that this is a normal condition. Technician B says that the system is overcharged. Who is right?
    A. Technician A only
    B. Technician B only
    C. Both A and B
    D. Neither A nor B   (A2)

15. All of the following statements about nitrogen flushing the A/C system are true **EXCEPT:**
    A. the technician should install a pressure regulator on the supply tank.
    B. the technician should disconnect the A/C compressor.
    C. the technician should remove restrictive components (i.e., STV, TXV valve) from the system.
    D. nitrogen must not be allowed to escape into the atmosphere.   (B1.7)

16. The LEAST likely cause of the high-pressure relief valve operating is:
    A. improper radiator shutter operation.
    B. a clogged condenser.
    C. inoperative cooling fan clutch.
    D. a defective A/C compressor.   (B2.1)

17. A cracked A/C compressor mounting plate could cause all of the following symptoms **EXCEPT:**
    A. drive belt wear.
    B. internal compressor damage.
    C. vibration with the A/C compressor clutch engaged.
    D. drive belt squeal or chatter.   (B2.7)

18. The test for non-condensable gases in recovered/recycled refrigerant involves:
    A. comparing the pressure of the recovered refrigerant in the container to the theoretical pressure of pure refrigerant at a given temperature.
    B. comparing the atmospheric pressure to the relative humidity.
    C. comparing the container pressure with the size of the container.
    D. testing the refrigerant with a halogen leak detector.   (E5)

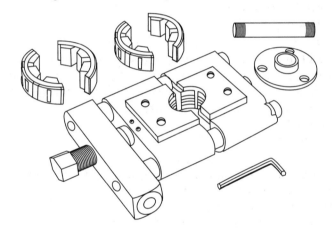

19. What tool or piece of equipment is shown in the figure above?
    A. Spring lock installation tool
    B. Bearing puller
    C. Hose end crimping tool
    D. Flare tool   (B3.2)

20. Technician A says that as specified by SAE J1991, recycled refrigerant cannot contain more than 15 ppm moisture contaminants by weight. Technician B says that as specified by SAE J1991, recycled refrigerant cannot contain more than 330 ppm non-condensable gases (air) by weight. Who is right?
    A. Technician A only
    B. Technician B only
    C. Both A and B
    D. Neither A nor B   (E3)

21. The best tool to use when troubleshooting a circuit with solid-state components is:
    A. a digital multimeter (DMM).
    B. a self-powered test lamp.
    C. an analog volt/ohmmeter.
    D. a 12V test lamp.   (D3.7)

22. A typical ATC system will delay blower motor operation until the coolant temperature reaches:
    A. 90°F (49°C).
    B. 70°F (38°C).
    C. 100°F (49°C).
    D. 120°F (32°C).   (D3.2)

23. Technician A says most fully automatic temperature control systems have some form of self-diagnostic program that will display trouble codes. Technician B says that depending on the system design, these codes may be displayed digitally on the control assembly or on a hand-held scan tool. Who is right?
    A. Technician A only
    B. Technician B only
    C. Both A and B
    D. Neither A nor B   (D3.1)

24. Approximately how much refrigerant oil must be added to a newly replaced evaporator core?
    A. None
    B. 3 ounces
    C. 9 ounces
    D. 14.5 ounces   (B3.8)

25. Technician A says that the best way to test a vacuum-operated coolant control valve is to disconnect the vacuum hose and observe whether coolant flows through it. Technician B says that the best way to test a vacuum-operated coolant control valve is to apply and release vacuum and check if the valve arm moves freely both ways. Who is right?
    A. Technician A only
    B. Technician B only
    C. Both A and B
    D. Neither A nor B   (C11)

26. A pressure tester can be used to test:
    A. thermostats.
    B. radiators, pressure caps, and hoses.
    C. for A/C leaks.
    D. the blend door actuator diaphragm.   (C5)

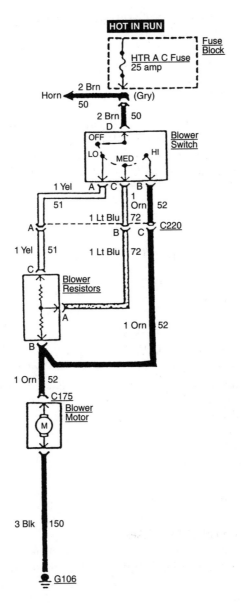

27. Refer to the figure shown above. The blower motor works in LO and HIGH positions but does not work on MED. Technician A says the problem could be an open blower resistor. Technician B says the problem could be the blower motor switch. Who is right?
    A. Technician A only
    B. Technician B only
    C. Both A and B
    D. Neither A nor B   (D1.2)

28. To check for cooling system leaks, pressurize the system and:
    A. use a black light to find leaks.
    B. use a leak detector to find leaks.
    C. perform a visual inspection.
    D. watch for white smoke.   (C3)

29. In an ATC system, a grinding noise comes from under the dash when the temperature setting is changed from WARM to COLD. The most likely cause of this problem is:
   A. grit in the evaporator case.
   B. a faulty mode door actuator.
   C. bad drive gears in the blend door motor.
   D. arcing in the control head.   (D3.5)

30. A spring inside the lower radiator hose is used to:
   A. pre-form the hose.
   B. prevent the hose from collapsing.
   C. make the hose more resilient.
   D. strengthen the hose.   (C4)

31. A routine A/C maintenance service should include all of the following **EXCEPT:**
   A. tightening the condenser lines.
   B. removing debris from the condenser fins.
   C. straightening the condenser fins.
   D. checking the condenser mounts.   (B3.4)

32. Flushing the cooling system does not:
   A. remove rust from the system.
   B. remove contaminants from the system.
   C. increase the life of the cooling system.
   D. remove acids of combustion from the cooling system.   (C8)

33. The expansion valve is located at:
   A. the inlet line of the evaporator.
   B. the outlet line of the evaporator.
   C. the inlet line of the compressor.
   D. the outlet line of the condenser.   (B3.6)

34. When replacing the heater core, foam tape is used:
   A. to insulate the heater core.
   B. to reduce noise from coolant surges.
   C. to protect and seal around the heater core.
   D. to seal the heater hose connections.   (C12)

35. Technician A says that the refrigerant containers for R-12 and R-134a are color coded. Technician B says that the R-134a containers use 1/2 inch, 16 ACME threads which cannot be mistakenly 'hooked up' to an R-12 gauge set or recovery machine. Who is right?
   A. Technician A only
   B. Technician B only
   C. Both A and B
   D. Neither A nor B   (B1.2)

36. When refilling an empty cooling system:
    A. always add the antifreeze before adding the water.
    B. always add the water before adding the antifreeze.
    C. always premix the antifreeze and water.
    D. always follow the manufacturer's instructions for bleeding the system.   (C8)

37. A cooling fan clutch can be controlled by any of the following **EXCEPT:**
    A. air.
    B. a thermostatic spring.
    C. changing viscosity of fan clutch fluid.
    D. a hydraulic switch.   (C10)

38. Technician A says that you can test the A/C compressor clutch coil with an ohmmeter. Technician B says that connecting battery power to one terminal of the coil and grounding the other terminal can test the A/C compressor clutch coil. Who is right?
    A. Technician A only
    B. Technician B only
    C. Both A and B
    D. Neither A nor B   (B2.4)

39. Technician A says that an electronic blend door motor uses a feedback device to indicate the position of the door. Technician B says that an electronic mode door motor uses a feedback device to indicate the position of the door. Who is right?
    A. Technician A only
    B. Technician B only
    C. Both A and B
    D. Neither A nor B   (D1.1)

40. Technician A says that the compressor oil needs to be checked when there is evidence of a loss of system oil. Technician B says that when replacing refrigerant oil, it is important to use the specific type and quantity of oil recommended by the compressor manufacturer. Who is right?
    A. Technician A only
    B. Technician B only
    C. Both A and B
    D. Neither A nor B   (B1.9)

41. Technician A says that many trucks are equipped with an engine shut-down alarm to warn the driver if coolant level and temperature are not within preset parameters. Technician B says that engine shut down can be overridden for a brief period after the alarm to allow the driver to move the vehicle to a safe place. Who is right?
    A. Technician A only
    B. Technician B only
    C. Both A and B
    D. Neither A nor B   (D1.5)

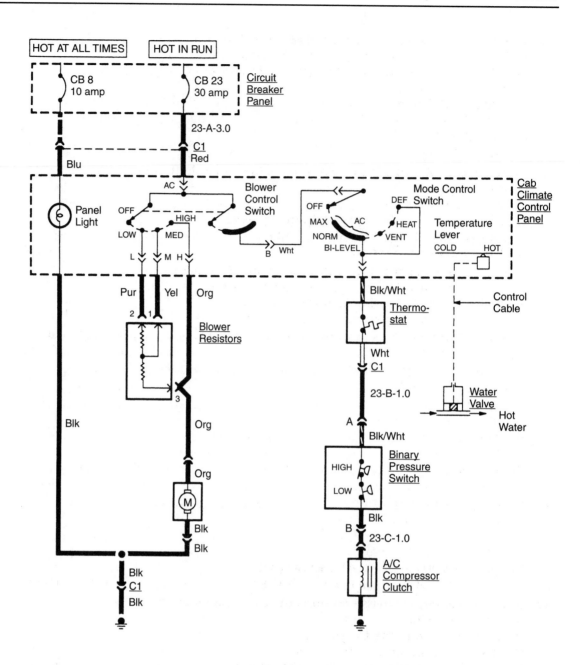

42. Refer to the figure shown above. All of the following could prevent A/C compressor clutch engagement **EXCEPT:**
    A. a defective blower switch.
    B. an open binary pressure switch.
    C. a poor connection at the A/C thermostat.
    D. a blown 10 amp fuse at CB 8.   (B2.4)

43. Technician A says that anyone who purchases R-134a must maintain records for three years indicating the name and address of the supplier. Technician B says the supplier must maintain these records. Who is right?
    A. Technician A only
    B. Technician B only
    C. Both A and B
    D. Neither A nor B   (E1)

44. Technician A says that the A/C compressor high-pressure relief valve must be replaced if it operates due to extreme pressure in the A/C system. Technician B says that the compressor must be replaced if the high-pressure relief valve operates. Who is right?
    A. Technician A only
    B. Technician B only
    C. Both A and B
    D. Neither A nor B   (B3.11)

45. Which of the following is the LEAST likely cause of a shutter system that will not close completely?
    A. A blown shutter fuse
    B. An air leak in the hose to the shutter cylinder
    C. Dirt accumulation on the shutter linkage
    D. Ice build-up on the shutters   (C13)

46. The easiest way to check the calibration of an ATC system is to:
    A. use an ohmmeter to measure the resistance of the ATC sensor.
    B. measure the voltage drop across the ATC sensor.
    C. turn the calibration screw on the ATC control unit.
    D. use a thermometer to measure the cab temperature and compare the actual temperature to the set temperature.   (D3.8)

47. All of the following statements about air controlled HVAC systems in heavy-duty trucks are true **EXCEPT:**
    A. the replacement of cables with small air lines facilitates the replacement of the HVAC control panel.
    B. coolant control valves cannot be controlled using chassis air.
    C. air cylinders are used to control mode and blend air doors.
    D. air leaks may cause mode doors to move slowly or to be totally inoperative.   (D2.3)

48. In an ATC system, the blend air door constantly moves back and forth. The most likely cause of this problem is:
    A. a binding blend air door.
    B. a faulty actuator motor.
    C. an improperly adjusted ATC sensor cable.
    D. a faulty actuator assembly feedback device.   (D3.3)

49. Before removing any chassis air hose, the technician must:
    A. start the engine.
    B. drain water from the air system.
    C. drain all of the air from the system.
    D. remove the air compressor from the vehicle.   (D2.6)

50. Technician A says that the HVAC systems on most medium-duty trucks with gasoline engines operate totally independent from the engine control system. Technician B says that most of the HVAC systems on these vehicles provide inputs and receive outputs from the engine control unit. Who is right?
    A. Technician A only
    B. Technician B only
    C. Both A and B
    D. Neither A nor B   (D1.4)

51. A faint ether-like odor coming from the panel vents in the NORMAL A/C mode could indicate:
    A. the evaporator core is leaking R-134a.
    B. the evaporator core is leaking R-12.
    C. the cold starting system is malfunctioning.
    D. the heater core is leaking.   (A2)

52. A/C compressor drive belt edge wear could indicate any of the following conditions **EXCEPT:**
   A. a bent or cracked compressor mounting bracket.
   B. improperly set compressor clutch air gap.
   C. a damaged compressor pulley.
   D. a worn idler pulley bearing.   (B2.3)

53. The A/C condenser has several bent fins and a moderate accumulation of dead insects. Technician A says that the condenser should be replaced or it will cause the high-pressure relief valve to operate. Technician B says that the condenser fins should be straightened and the dead insects removed to optimize A/C system performance. Who is right?
   A. Technician A only
   B. Technician B only
   C. Both A and B
   D. Neither A nor B   (B3.3)

54. A check valve is installed in-line to the vacuum reservoir to:
   A. delay vacuum to downstream components.
   B. switch vacuum on and off to various components.
   C. prevent a vacuum drop during periods of low-source vacuum.
   D. monitor engine vacuum.   (D2.5)

55. Which of the following is a typical heavy-duty truck cooling system operating pressure?
   A. 3 psi
   B. 15 psi
   C. 20 psi
   D. 30 psi   (C5)

56. A vacuum operated blend door actuator diaphragm:
   A. is designed to bleed vacuum at a rate of 3 in. Hg. per hour.
   B. contains a small electric motor to return the actuator to the normal position.
   C. should hold vacuum indefinitely.
   D. is porous to allow moisture to evaporate.   (D2.4)

57. Technician A says that the best way to repair wiring in the compressor clutch circuit is by soldering. Technician B says that twisting the wires together and securing them with electrical tape is sufficient. Who is right?
   A. Technician A only
   B. Technician B only
   C. Both A and B
   D. Neither A nor B   (D1.3)

58. A technician finds the HVAC control panel as the source of a chassis air leak. The best method of repair is:
   A. replacement of the control panel.
   B. replacement of the pintle O-rings.
   C. re-packing the selector body with grease.
   D. replacing the selector levers.   (D2.2)

59. The A/C high pressure switch is used to:
   A. boost the system high-side pressure.
   B. open the circuit to the A/C compressor clutch coil when the high-side pressure reaches its upper limit.
   C. ensure that system pressure remains at the upper limit.
   D. vent refrigerant from the compressor in the event of extremely high system pressure.   (B2.2)

60. Filters installed in the HVAC air delivery system:
    A. are always made of fiberglass mesh to resist corrosion.
    B. are designed to remove moisture from cab and sleeper air.
    C. are not individually replaceable.
    D. are designed to remove dust and dirt from cab and sleeper air.   (B3.9)

61. Inadequate air flow from one or more vents could be caused by:
    A. a misaligned air duct.
    B. a faulty blower resistor.
    C. a clogged heater core.
    D. high ambient humidity.   (D2.7)

62. When the engine cooling fan clutch is disengaged:
    A. the fan blade will remain stationary.
    B. the engine idle will drop.
    C. the radiator shutters must be closed.
    D. the fan blade may freewheel at a reduced speed.   (C10)

63. All of the following can cause the air pressure regulator to 'pop-off' frequently
    EXCEPT:
    A. a defective compressor unloader assembly.
    B. a faulty automatic water drain.
    C. a weak regulator control spring.
    D. a defective compressor governor.   (D2.6)

64. While inspecting the chassis air system, a technician finds the radiator shutter
    cylinder to be leaking. Technician A says you must replace the cylinder. Technician
    B says you must overhaul the cylinder. Who is right?
    A. Technician A only
    B. Technician B only
    C. Both A and B
    D. Neither A nor B   (C13)

65. The LEAST likely cause of poor coolant circulation is:
    A. a defective thermostat.
    B. an eroded water pump impeller.
    C. a collapsed upper radiator hose.
    D. a collapsed lower radiator hose.   (C6)

66. With the selector lever in the MAX A/C position, a blend air HVAC system outputs
    cold air for about 15 minutes, at which time the output air becomes warm. The
    most likely cause of this problem is:
    A. a defective thermal expansion valve.
    B. a defective coolant control valve.
    C. a defective blend air door return spring.
    D. a defective fresh air door.   (B1.1)

67. The A/C compressor clutch will not engage in any mode. The clutch engages
    when a technician installs a jumper wire across the terminals of the low-pressure
    cut-out switch connector. Technician A says that the low pressure cut-out switch
    must be defective. Technician B says that the refrigerant charge might be low.
    Who is right?
    A. Technician A only
    B. Technician B only
    C. Both A and B
    D. Neither A nor B   (B2.1)

68. How much refrigeration oil should be in a typical A/C condenser?
    A. One ounce
    B. Five ounces
    C. Seven ounces
    D. Eleven ounces   (B3.1)

69. When pressure testing a cooling system, there are no obvious leaks but the system cannot maintain pressure. The most likely cause of this problem is:
    A. leaking evaporator.
    B. a leaking power steering cooler.
    C. a leaking oil cooler.
    D. a blown head gasket in the engine.   (C3)

70. Before replacing an electric blend air door actuator, the technician should:
    A. ensure that the batteries are removed from the vehicle.
    B. ensure that the batteries have a good ground.
    C. ensure that the blend door moves freely.
    D. ground himself to the vehicle.   (D1.6)

71. What is the LEAST likely cause of an inoperative HVAC mode switch?
    A. Vacuum leak
    B. Air leak
    C. Broken cable
    D. Open blower resistor   (D2.1)

72. Technician A says that many ATC systems use a microprocessor that is built into the control panel. Technician B says that some ATC systems use a microprocessor that can be replaced independently from the control panel. Who is right?
    A. Technician A only
    B. Technician B only
    C. Both A and B
    D. Neither A nor B   (D3.7)

73. Which of these characteristics does the R-134a refrigerant possess?
    A. Is odorless
    B. Has a faint ether-like odor
    C. Has a strong rotten egg odor
    D. Has a cabbage-like odor   (B1.2)

74. All of the following statements about checking the A/C compressor lubricant level are true **EXCEPT:**
    A. the A/C system must first be completely evacuated.
    B. the compressor must not be operated for at least 24 hours before checking the lubricant level.
    C. the compressor must be removed from the vehicle.
    D. the old lubricant must be measured before new lubricant is added.   (B2.5)

75. Technician A says that when installing new A/C hose O-rings, a seal pick should be used to minimize skin contact with the new seal. Technician B says that the petroleum jelly used to lubricate the new O-rings will protect them from the oils in the skin. Who is right?
    A. Technician A only
    B. Technician B only
    C. Both A and B
    D. Neither A nor B   (B3.2)

76. Cooling and heating system hoses should be replaced for any of the following reasons **EXCEPT:**
    A. they appear to be old.
    B. they are cracked.
    C. they show signs of bulging.
    D. they feel spongy.   (C4)

77. An electric condenser fan may be controlled by any of the following **EXCEPT:**
    A. the engine control unit.
    B. the body control unit.
    C. a manual switch.
    D. an electronic relay.   (D1.5)

78. Which of the following is the LEAST likely cause of a binding temperature control cable?
    A. A kinked cable housing
    B. Corrosion in the cable housing
    C. A deformed or overtightened cable clamp
    D. A fault mode door   (D2.3)

79. Which of the following statements about coolant control valve replacement in an ATC system is true?
    A. The refrigerant must be evacuated before the coolant control valve is replaced.
    B. The heater hoses connected to the coolant control valve may be clamped during the replacement procedure to maintain coolant in the system.
    C. Access to the coolant control valve is gained through the fresh air door.
    D. The coolant control valve is an integral part of the heater hose.   (D3.4)

80. Any of the following can be used to clean road debris from the condenser fins **EXCEPT:**
    A. a mild saline solution.
    B. a soft whisk broom.
    C. compressed air.
    D. a mild soap and water solution.   (B3.3)

81. The thermal bulb on an expansion valve must be installed in contact with:
    A. the evaporator inlet or core.
    B. the condenser fins.
    C. the suction hose.
    D. the refrigerant.   (B3.6)

82. The driver of a truck discovers a heater core leak in the sleeper that needs replacement. Technician A says that it is important to add the proper amount of refrigeration oil before installation. Technician B says that a PAG-based lubricant is used in modern heater cores. Who is right?
    A. Technician A only
    B. Technician B only
    C. Both A and B
    D. Neither A nor B   (C.12)

83. While checking an ATC system with a hand-held scan tool, the ATC microprocessor generates a fault code with a failure mode identifier (FMI) of 12. The technician should:
    A. look for an open wire.
    B. look for a short circuit to ground.
    C. replace the control module.
    D. look for a loose connector.   (D3.7)

84. Before replacing an HVAC electrical control panel, the technician should:
    A. remove the control cables from the vehicle.
    B. disconnect the battery.
    C. disassemble the dash panel.
    D. apply dielectric grease to the switch contacts.   (D1.7)

85. A blown HVAC system fuse could indicate any of the following **EXCEPT:**
    A. a short circuit to ground in the blower circuit.
    B. a short circuit to ground in the blend door actuator.
    C. a short circuit in the engine coolant temperature sensor (ECT).
    D. a damaged wiring harness connector.   (D1.1)

86. The moisture sensor in Red Dot Refrigeration Management Systems (RMS™) is cobalt blue. Technician A says that there is moisture in the A/C system and you replace the receiver/drier. Technician B says that you can remove the moisture in the system by evacuating the A/C system. Who is right?
    A. Technician A only
    B. Technician B only
    C. Both A and B
    D. Neither A nor B   (B3.5)

87. Overtightening the mounting screws of an HVAC system vacuum actuator can result in:
    A. a ruptured diaphragm.
    B. stripped screw holes.
    C. deformed linkage.
    D. a vacuum leak.   (B2.4)

88. The A/C compressor high-pressure relief valve:
    A. is calibrated by shimming it to the proper depth.
    B. must be replaced if it ever vents refrigerant from the system.
    C. will reset itself when A/C system pressure returns to a safe level.
    D. is not used in R-134a systems.   (B3.11)

89. A customer complains that his air operated heater outputs hot air when the temperature control lever is in the COLD position. The LEAST likely cause of this problem is:
    A. a defective coolant control valve.
    B. a defective engine coolant temperature sensor.
    C. a defective air control solenoid.
    D. a defective blend air door control cylinder.   (D2.1)

90. The refrigerant in an A/C system quickly changes state from liquid to vapor as it flows through the:
    A. vapor line.
    B. condenser.
    C. fixed orifice.
    D. capillary tube.   (B3.7)

91. Technician A says a suction throttling valve not regulating properly could cause reduced air flow from the instrument panel outlets. Technician B says a suction throttling valve not regulating properly could cause the evaporator to ice up. Who is right?
    A. Technician A only
    B. Technician B only
    C. Both A and B
    D. Neither A nor B   (B2.1)

92. Which cab heating system is the most common type used in trucks?
    A. Forced air convection heater
    B. Immersion heater
    C. Fuel-fired heater
    D. Electric heater   (A3)

93. Refrigerant recovery and storage cylinders must be Department of Transportation (DOT) approved. What level of approval is necessary for refrigerant recovery containers?
    A. DOT 39-300
    B. DOT 4BA-300
    C. DOT 4BC-400
    D. DOT 3DE-500   (E4)

94. While testing an A/C system at normal speed and temperature, the high- and low-side pressure are the same. Technician A says the clutch is not engaged. Technician B says there is a restriction in the expansion valve. Who is right?
    A. Technician A only
    B. Technician B only
    C. Both A and B
    D. Neither A nor B   (B1.3)

95. Mobile A/C systems using R-12 have flared and threaded service ports, with the port size differentiating high side from low side. Service fittings on systems with R-134a use:
    A. compression fittings.
    B. SAE approved quick-connect couplings.
    C. The same fittings as R-12 systems.
    D. 10 mm threaded ports.   (E2)

96. To prevent overfilling of recovery cylinders, the service technician must:
    A. monitor cylinder pressure as the cylinder is being filled.
    B. monitor cylinder weight as the cylinder is being filled.
    C. make sure cylinder safety relief valves are in place and operational.
    D. occasionally shake the cylinder and observe any change of pressure while filling.   (E2)

97. When evacuating an A/C system, the vacuum pump should be operated a minimum of:
    A. 20 minutes.
    B. 10 minutes.
    C. 15 minutes.
    D. 30 minutes.   (B1.6)

98. Which of the following gases is most important for shielding the earth from ultraviolet radiation?
    A. Methane
    B. Stratospheric ozone
    C. Nitrogen
    D. Argon   (E3)

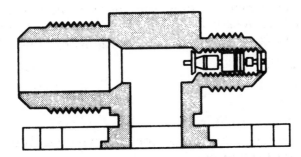

99. Technician A says that when servicing a system with the type of service valve shown in the figure above, the compressor cannot be isolated. Technician B says that the valve shown in the figure above permits reading of the suction and discharge pressures without having to manually front seat or back seat. Who is right?
    A. Technician A only
    B. Technician B only
    C. Both A and B
    D. Neither A nor B   (B2.6)

100. If R-12 comes into contact with a flame:
    A. it will explode.
    B. it will form a non-toxic gas.
    C. it will form chlorine crystals.
    D. it will form phosgene gas.   (E4)

101. The refrigerant line leading from the evaporator to the compressor contains refrigerant as a:
    A. low pressure gas.
    B. low pressure liquid.
    C. high pressure gas.
    D. high pressure liquid.   (A3)

102. Purging a system too fast will result in:
    A. phosgene gas formation.
    B. oil being drawn from the compressor.
    C. reed valve damage.
    D. receiver/drier damage.   (B1.6)

103. In MAX A/C mode:
    A. the outside air door is closed.
    B. the defroster door is open.
    C. the compressor clutch cannot disengage.
    D. the blower is disabled.   (B1.3)

104. On a cycling clutch A/C system, the low side reading is too high and the high side reading is too low. Technician A says that the compressor may have an internal leak. Technician B says that an overcharge of refrigerant oil is a possible cause. Who is right?
    A. Technician A only
    B. Technician B only
    C. Both A and B
    D. Neither A nor B   (B1.3)

105. A/C system pressures vary with all of the following **EXCEPT:**
    A. altitude.
    B. ambient temperature.
    C. barometric pressure.
    D. cab temperature.   (B1.3)

106. In mobile A/C systems, evaporator core icing can be prevented by any of the following **EXCEPT:**
    A. a thermostatic switch.
    B. an EPR valve.
    C. an STV.
    D. a low pressure cut-off switch.   (D1.3)

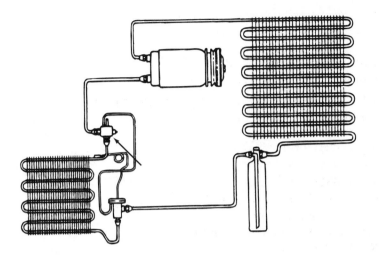

107. The arrow shown in the figure above is pointing to the:
    A. thermostatic expansion valve (TXV).
    B. valve in receiver (VIR) unit.
    C. evaporator pressure regulator (EPR).
    D. suction throttling valve (STV).   (A3)

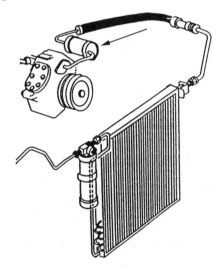

108. The arrow shown in the figure above is pointing to the:
    A. pilot operated absolute (POA) valve.
    B. filter.
    C. evaporator temperature regulator (ETR).
    D. muffler.   (A3)

109. A binary pressure switch provides which of the following:
    A. only low pressure protection for the A/C system.
    B. only high pressure protection for the A/C system.
    C. both low and high pressure protection for the A/C system.
    D. neither low pressure nor high pressure protection for the A/C system.   (B2.2)

110. A restricted orifice tube will reduce the cooling ability of an A/C system because of which of the following functions of the orifice tube:
    A. it allows water to drain from the evaporator case.
    B. it allows rapid expansion of high pressure liquid refrigerant.
    C. it regulates refrigerant flow through the condenser.
    D. it regulates air flow through the evaporator.   (B3.7)

111. On accumulator-type systems with the compressor cycling switch located on the accumulator, the switch measures:
    A. outside temperature.
    B. accumulator pressure.
    C. accumulator temperature.
    D. engine compartment temperature.   (D1.3)

112. An A/C system with excessive high-side pressure could be the result of all of the following **EXCEPT:**
    A. an overcharge of refrigerant.
    B. an overheated engine.
    C. restricted air flow through the condenser.
    D. ice building up on the orifice tube screen.   (B1.3)

113. To detect a refrigerant leak, hold the leak detector sensor:
    A. within three inches of the fitting.
    B. just below the fitting.
    C. right next to the fitting.
    D. just above the fitting.   (B1.5)

114. A compressor cycling on and off too fast is one symptom of:
    A. a defective compressor clutch.
    B. a defective control switch.
    C. an overcharged system.
    D. a low refrigerant charge.   (B1.4)

115. If one of the reed valves fails in an A/C compressor, the result is low cooling because of which of these compressor reed valve functions:
    A. stays open when the compressor is hot.
    B. maintains a certain temperature.
    C. maintains a certain pressure.
    D. directs the flow of refrigerant.   (B2.6)

116. If a retrofit from R-12 to R-134a is to be performed, the technician should first read the appropriate service information to:
    A. find the manufacturer's procedures for retrofitting.
    B. confirm that the vehicle has an R-12 system.
    C. confirm the vehicle warranty status.
    D. discover what parts of the system have been replaced over the vehicle's service life.   (B1.2)

117. Which of the following modes will affect windshield defrosting in the DEFROST mode:
    A. 50% of the output air is directed to the floor and 50% to the windshield.
    B. 15% of the output air is directed to the floor and 85% to the windshield.
    C. 25% of the output air is directed to the floor and 75% to the windshield.
    D. 30% of the output air is directed to the floor and 70% to the windshield.   (A3)

118. Which method of detecting refrigerant leaks is most precise?
    A. Looking for bubbles after spraying with a soapy solution
    B. Using an electronic leak detector
    C. Using a flame-type leak detector
    D. Using a black light detector   (B1.5)

119. If the expansion valve is not opening, the system will show which of the following pressure combinations on a manifold gauge set:
    A. low, low-side pressure and low, high-side pressure.
    B. low, low-side pressure and high, high-side pressure.
    C. high, low-side pressure and high, high-side pressure.
    D. high, low-side pressure and low, high-side pressure.   (B1.3)

120. If the blower does not operate at medium speed, the problem is most likely:
    A. an open resistor.
    B. an intermittent short in the blower motor.
    C. a loose contact in the blower switch.
    D. a loose terminal in the connector.　　　　　　　　　　(D1.2)

121. A faint hissing noise is heard from the area of the evaporator immediately after shutting down the engine with the compressor clutch engaged. Technician A says that the A/C system has a leak. Technician B says the evaporator pressure regulator is defective. Who is right?
    A. Technician A only
    B. Technician B only
    C. Both A and B
    D. Neither A nor B　　　　　　　　　　(A1)

122. Technician A says that fuel-fired heaters are rather new to the United States. Technician B says that fuel-fired heaters burn less fuel than idling the engine. Who is right?
    A. Technician A only
    B. Technician B only
    C. Both A and B
    D. Neither A nor B　　　　　　　　　　(A3)

123. The most common problem with mobile HVAC systems is:
    A. clogged heater cores.
    B. defective control units.
    C. faulty control valves.
    D. coolant leaks.　　　　　　　　　　(C1)

124. All of the following are a type of mobile HVAC system **EXCEPT:**
    A. blend air type.
    B. automatic temperature control (ATC).
    C. recirculating chilled and heated water .
    D. semi-automatic temperature control (SATC).　　　　　　　　　　(A3)

125. Before disposing of an empty or near empty original container that was used to ship refrigerant from the factory you should perform which of the following:
    A. clean it and keep it for storage of recycled refrigerant.
    B. open the valve completely and paint an X on the cylinder.
    C. flush it with oil and nitrogen to keep it from rusting.
    D. recover remaining refrigerant, evacuate cylinder, and mark it empty.　　(E4)

126. Technician A says that the manifold gauge set is the only tool needed to diagnose HVAC systems. Technician B says a small thermometer is a valuable tool to evaluate the performance of an HVAC system. Who is right?
    A. Technician A only
    B. Technician B only
    C. Both A and B
    D. Neither A nor B　　　　　　　　　　(A3)

127. Of the following, which is a normal low-side gauge operating pressure?
    A. 5–10 psi
    B. 25–45 psi
    C. 60–80 psi
    D. 180–205 psi　　　　　　　　　　(B1.3)

128. Oil and dirt accumulation on an A/C hose connection may indicate:
    A. excessive pressure in the system.
    B. a refrigerant leak.
    C. a defective compressor shaft seal.
    D. that there is too much oil in the system.　　　　　　　　　　(B1.4)

129. Technician A says a system having high, low-side pressure accompanied by a continuously running compressor indicates that the expansion valve is stuck open. Technician B says a system having a high, low-side reading accompanied by a continuously running compressor indicates that the expansion valve is operating properly. Who is right?
     A. Technician A only
     B. Technician B only
     C. Both A and B
     D. Neither A nor B
     (B1.3)

130. During an HVAC performance test, the technician hears the A/C compressor clutch slip briefly upon engagement. The most likely cause is:
     A. a worn out compressor clutch coil.
     B. a defective A/C compressor clutch relay.
     C. the compressor clutch air gap is too large.
     D. the compressor clutch bearing is worn.
     (A1)

131. While conducting a performance test on a semi-automatic HVAC system, a technician finds that only a small amount of air is directed to the windshield in DEFROST mode. The most likely cause of this problem is:
     A. a defective microprocessor.
     B. a defective blend door actuator.
     C. an open blower motor resistor.
     D. a improperly adjusted mode door cable.
     (A3)

132. A screen is located in the orifice tube of an A/C system. Technician A says that the screen is a filter used to prevent particulate from circulating through the system. Technician B says that the screen is used to improve atomization of the refrigerant. Who is right?
     A. Technician A only
     B. Technician B only
     C. Both A and B
     D. Neither A nor B
     (B3.7)

133. The compressor discharge valve is designed to:
     A. open after the vaporous refrigerant is compressed, allowing the refrigerant to move to the condenser.
     B. open before the vaporous refrigerant is compressed, allowing the refrigerant to move to the evaporator.
     C. regulate system variable pressure.
     D. regulate A/C system temperature.
     (B2.6)

134. Technician A says that the evaporator must be removed from the vehicle if the evaporator lubricant level is to be checked. Technician B says that first you run the A/C compressor briefly to ensure that the refrigeration oil distributes throughout the system. Who is right?
     A. Technician A only
     B. Technician B only
     C. Both A and B
     D. Neither A nor B
     (B3.1)

135. Which of the following items is most likely to cause elevated high-side pressure in an A/C system?
     A. Restricted air flow through condenser.
     B. A thermostat stuck open
     C. A leaking thermal bulb.
     D. An open bypass valve   (B1.3)

136. Technician A says that it is not important to remove moisture from the A/C system before charging the system. Technician B says moisture that enters the A/C system will be harmful to the system and cause poor performance. Who is right?
     A. Technician A only
     B. Technician B only
     C. Both A and B
     D. Neither A nor B   (B1.6)

137. Technician A says some manufacturers recommend the installation of an in-line filter between the evaporator and the compressor as an alternative to refrigerant system flushing. Technician B says an in-line filter containing a fixed orifice may be installed and the original orifice tube left in the system. Who is right?
     A. Technician A only
     B. Technician B only
     C. Both A and B
     D. Neither A nor B   (B1.7)

138. Technician A says you can complete the high-side charging procedure with the engine running. Technician B says if liquid refrigerant enters the compressor, damage will result to the compressor. Who is right?
     A. Technician A only
     B. Technician B only
     C. Both A and B
     D. Neither A nor B   (B1.8)

139. A heavy-duty truck is about to have the A/C system recharged, which of these items is correct concerning that process:
     A. One completes the charging process when the system reaches the correct evaporator temperature.
     B. When the low side no longer moves from a vacuum to a pressure, the process is complete.
     C. The truck engine must be running during recharging.
     D. You can use either a high-side or a low-side charging process.   (B1.8)

140. Technician A says all A/C systems use a mineral based internal lubricant. Technician B says PAG oil is a non-synthetic form of lubricant. Who is right?
     A. Technician A only
     B. Technician B only
     C. Both A and B
     D. Neither A nor B   (B1.9)

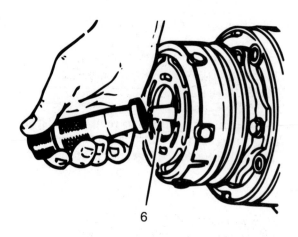

6

141. Technician A says component 6 in the figure above is a seal protector that one places over the compressor shaft. Technician B says you must install the seal seat O-ring before the compressor shaft seal. Who is right?
    A. Technician A only
    B. Technician B only
    C. Both A and B
    D. Neither A nor B
                                                                                (B2.7)

142. The inside of a truck windshield has an oily film and the A/C cooling is poor. Technician A says a plugged HVAC heater case drain may cause this oil film. Technician B says this film may be caused by a leak in the evaporator case. Who is right?
    A. Technician A only
    B. Technician B only
    C. Both A and B
    D. Neither A nor B
                                                                                (B3.8)

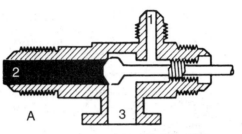

Front-Seated Position

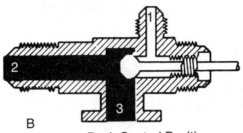

Back-Seated Position

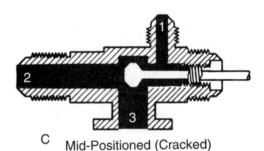

C   Mid-Positioned (Cracked)

143. With a stem type service valve in the position shown in the figure above:
    A. You can diagnose the refrigerant system with a manifold gauge set.
    B. The refrigerant system operates normally with no pressure at the gauge ports.
    C. The refrigerant system is isolated from the compressor for compressor removal.
    D. The refrigerant system may be discharged, evacuated, and recharged.   (B3.10)

144. The inside of the windshield has a sticky film. Technician A says to check the engine coolant level. Technician B says the heater core may be leaking. Who is right?
    A. Technician A only
    B. Technician B only
    C. Both A and B
    D. Neither A nor B   (C2)

145. A 427 cubic inch gasoline engine in a school bus with indirect port fuel injection and air conditioning has an excessively rich air–fuel ratio. This problem could be caused by which of these items:
    A. engine overheating.
    B. a defective radiator cap.
    C. the engine thermostat stuck open.
    D. the coolant control valve stuck open.   (C7)

146. All of these statements about cooling system service are true **EXCEPT:**
    A. when the cooling system pressure is increased the boiling point increases.
    B. if one adds more antifreeze to the coolant, the boiling point decreases.
    C. a good quality ethylene glycol antifreeze contains antirust inhibitors.
    D. coolant solutions are recovered, recycled, and handled as hazardous waste.   (C8)

147. When checking the coolant condition with an SCA test strip, the technician finds that the coolant condition is higher than specification limits. Which of these items should the technician do?
    A. Add more antifreeze to increase the SCA.
    B. Continue to run the truck until the next PMI.
    C. Drain the entire coolant system and add the proper SCA mixture.
    D. Run the truck with no SCA additives until the next PMI.   (C9)

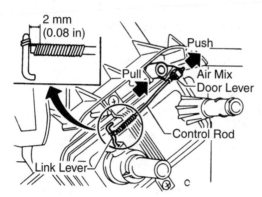

148. What adjustment is being performed in the figure above?
    A. The air mix door adjustment.
    B. The manual coolant valve adjustment.
    C. The ventilation door control rod adjustment.
    D. The defroster door control rod adjustment.   (C11)

149. A Diesel with a distributor-type fuel injection pump and throttle fast idle solenoid experiences a stalling problem when the A/C system compressor is engaged. Technician A says the throttle solenoid may be out of adjustment. Technician B says the engine computer may not be energizing the fast idle solenoid. Who is right?
    A. Technician A only
    B. Technician B only
    C. Both A and B
    D. Neither A nor B   (D1.4)

150. All of these facts about a computer controlled A/C system are correct **EXCEPT:**
    A. Some actuator motors are calibrated automatically in the self-diagnostic mode.
    B. A/C diagnostic trouble codes (DTC) represent a fault in a specific component.
    C. the actuator control rods must be calibrated manually on some systems.
    D. the actuator motor control rods should only require adjustment after motor replacement or adjustment.   (D1.6)

151. All of the statements about an HVAC control panel are true **EXCEPT:**
    A. you remove the negative battery cable before control panel service.
    B. you must discharge the refrigerant before removing the control panel.
    C. if the truck contains a Supplemental Restraint System, wait the specified period after you remove the negative battery cable.
    D. self-diagnostic tests may indicate a defective control panel in an ATC system.   (D1.7)

152. An HVAC system with a vacuum control panel experiences no cold air out of the dash nozzles, only out of the heat outlets. Which of these items is the most likely cause?
    A. A leaking dash vacuum switch
    B. A defective A/C compressor
    C. Loss of vacuum to the control panel
    D. A defective heater control valve   (D2.2)

153. Technician A says you test control panel vacuum systems by applying vacuum with a hand pump to the upstream (output) end of the system. Technician B says when you test connect a vacuum actuator the vacuum pump should stay at a steady vacuum for 1 minute with supply 15 to 20 inches supplied. Who is right?
    A. Technician A only
    B. Technician B only
    C. Both A and B
    D. Neither A nor B   (D2.4)

154. The driver of a gasoline powered truck notices that when the engine is turned off or the truck goes up hill, the air coming out of the A/C dash nozzles quickly shifts to the heater mode. Which of these could be the cause?
    A. A bad reservoir check valve
    B. A bad vacuum pump
    C. Bad fuel injectors
    D. Leaking actuator diaphragm   (D2.5)

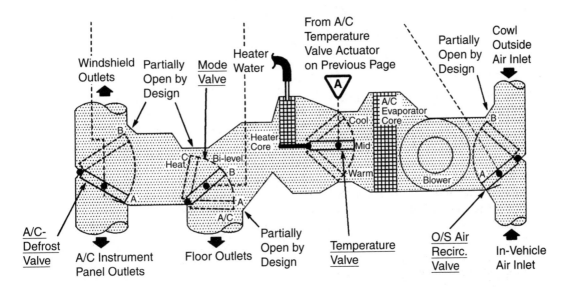

155. The outlet air recirculation door is stuck in position A in the figure above. Technician A says under this condition outside air is drawn into the HVAC case. Technician B says under this condition some in-vehicle air leaks past the doors. Who is right?
    A. Technician A only
    B. Technician B only
    C. Both A and B
    D. Neither A nor B   (D2.7)

156. In a ATC A/C system, the temperature control is set at 70°F (21°C), and the in-car temperature is 80°F (27°C) after driving one hour. All refrigerant pressures are normal. Technician A says the in-car sensor may be defective. Technician B says the temperature blend door may be sticking. Who is right?
    A. Technician A only
    B. Technician B only
    C. Both A and B
    D. Neither A nor   (D3.1)

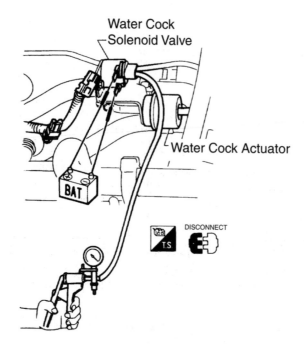

157. In the above figure vacuum is supplied from a hand pump to the water valve solenoid and battery voltage is furnished to the solenoid terminals resulting in an audible click. The system holds 16 inches of Hg. The water valve does not move. All of these defects may be the cause of the this problem, **EXCEPT:**
   A. A seized water control valve in the heater hose.
   B. a plugged vacuum hose between the solenoid and valve
   C. A jammed linkage from the actuator to the water drain.
   D. A seized plunger in the water valve control solenoid.   (D3.4)

158. When diagnosing a computer controlled ATC A/C system, a diagnostic trouble code is obtained indicating a fault in the temperature blend door actuator motor. Technician A says the first step in the repair process is to replace the temperature blend door actuator. Technician B says you need to check the temperature blend door for binding. Who is right?
   A. Technician A only
   B. Technician B only
   C. Both A and B
   D. Neither A nor B   (D3.5)

159. A diagnostic trouble code (DTC) representing the ambient sensor occurs in the circuit in the figure above. The ambient sensor and connector 2 are connected and connector 7 is disconnected from the ATC control panel. An ohmmeter connected to terminals 9 and 18 in the control panel connector indicates the specified resistance. The most likely cause of this DTC is:
   A. a defective ambient sensor.
   B. a defective A/C control panel.
   C. a loose connection at connector 2 and 7.
   D. an open connection at connector 7 terminal 18.   (D3.6)

160. An ATC control panel is suspected of causing an A/C performance problem in a tractor. Technician A says you should replace the ATC control computer. Technician B says you should follow and perform the diagnostic steps in the truck manufacturer's service manual. Who is right?
   A. Technician A only
   B. Technician B only
   C. Both A and B
   D. Neither A nor B   (D3.6)

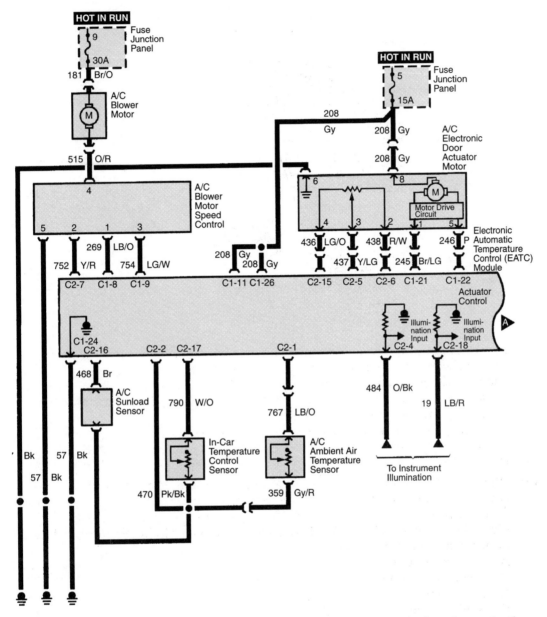

161. When measuring the voltage drop in the A/C computer ground as shown in the figure above, you connect a voltmeter from computer terminal C1-24 internal ground to the external ground. With the ignition on, the maximum voltage drop should be which of these items:

A. .1 volts.
B. .2 volts.
C. .5 volts.
D. .8 volts.

(D3.8)

162. All of these statements about A/C recovery/recycling equipment are true **EXCEPT:**
    A. the equipment label must indicate UL approval.
    B. the equipment label must indicate SAE J1991 approval.
    C. any size and type of refrigerant storage container over 10 lbs. may be used in this equipment.
    D. R-12 and R-134a refrigerants or refrigerant oils must not be mixed in the recovery/recycling process.   (E1)

163. The condenser changes:
    A. high pressure vapor into low pressure liquid.
    B. high pressure vapor into high pressure liquid.
    C. low pressure vapor into low pressure liquid.
    D. high pressure liquid into low pressure liquid.   (D3.3)

Appendices

Answers to the Test Questions for the Sample Test Section 5

1.	B	20.	D	39.	A	58.	D
2.	B	21.	B	40.	A	59.	D
3.	D	22.	C	41.	D	60.	A
4.	C	23.	A	42.	A	61.	C
5.	C	24.	B	43.	B	62.	D
6.	C	25.	D	44.	A	63.	A
7.	D	26.	B	45.	D	64.	A
8.	C	27.	A	46.	A	65.	D
9.	C	28.	A	47.	A	66.	C
10.	A	29.	D	48.	D	67.	B
11.	C	30.	C	49.	B	68.	A
12.	C	31.	A	50.	D	69.	D
13.	A	32.	C	51.	C	70.	A
14.	C	33.	D	52.	A	71.	A
15.	B	34.	B	53.	D		
16.	A	35.	B	54.	D		
17.	C	36.	A	55.	D		
18.	C	37.	B	56.	B		
19.	C	38.	A	57.	B		

Explanations to the Answers for the Sample Test Section 5

Question #1
Answer A is wrong because if the compressor bearing were the cause, the noise would only be present with the clutch engaged.
Answer B is correct because when the clutch engages, the outer race of the clutch bearing is stationary with respect to the inner race.
Answer C is wrong because only one technician is right.
Answer D is wrong because one of the technicians is right.

Question #2
Answer A is wrong because R-12 is an odorless gas.
Answer B is correct because the odor of leaking antifreeze can be drawn from the evaporator case even when operating in an A/C mode.
Answer C is wrong because only one technician is right.
Answer D is wrong because one of the technicians is right.

Question #3
Answer A is wrong because a low refrigerant charge will not affect heater temperature control.
Answer B is wrong because even with a very low coolant level, some cooling will take place with the A/C on.
Answer C is wrong because a compressor clutch failure will not affect heater temperature control.
Answer D is correct because a broken blend door cable will prevent the control of the HVAC system output air.

Question #4
Answer A is wrong because 20 in. Hg. is not sufficient to ensure that all moisture has been removed from the air in the tank.
Answer B is wrong because 22 in. Hg. is not sufficient to ensure that all moisture has been removed from the air in the tank.
Answer C is correct because 30 inches is required to remove all of the moisture from the system.
Answer D is wrong because 12 in. Hg. is not sufficient to ensure that all moisture has been removed from the air in the tank.

Question #5
Answer A is wrong because the blower uses three different resistance branches to achieve the different speeds, but in this switch position only one is used.
Answer B is wrong because the blower uses three different resistance branches to achieve the different speeds, but in the medium switch position only one, not two, are used.
Answer C is correct because only one resistor is used to achieve medium-2 position speed.
Answer D is wrong because the absence of resistance in the circuit would produce a high, not medium, speed. This is not shown in this figure.

Question #6
Answer A is wrong because a faulty circuit breaker will deny power to the system.
Answer B is wrong because ambient air temperature below 40°F will open the ambient cut-off switch, disabling the compressor clutch.
Answer C is correct because if the ambient cut-off switch is stuck closed, the compressor clutch is not disabled.
Answer D is wrong because an open black-yellow wire will disable the compressor clutch.

Question #7
Answer A is wrong because solvent can damage system components and is difficult to remove from the system.
Answer B is wrong because CFC refrigerants must never be used to flush the A/C system.
Answer C is wrong because for a filter to work, the particulate must circulate through the system, creating the potential for component damage or clogging.
Answer D is correct because nitrogen flushing will remove particulate before it can damage system components.

Question #8
Answer A is wrong because the size specified is incorrect.
Answer B is wrong because the size specified is incorrect.
Answer C is correct because the size specified is correct.
Answer D is wrong because the size specified is incorrect.

Question #9
Answer A is wrong because a clogged heater core could also cause the problem.
Answer B is wrong because an improperly adjusted temperature control cable could also cause the problem.
Answer C is correct because both technicians are correct.
Answer D is wrong because one of the technicians is right.

Question #10
Answer A is correct because the low pressure cut-out switch senses high-side pressure and disables the compressor clutch in the event of a low refrigerant charge.
Answer B is wrong because an aneroid or a BAP sensor senses atmospheric pressure.
Answer C is wrong because low-side pressure would not drop fast enough on a low refrigerant charge and if the ambient temperature is high, the pressure on the low side would be high.
Answer D is wrong because there is not generally a sensor for cab/sleeper pressure.

Question #11
Answer A is wrong because the high pressure hose is connected to the high-side service valve.
Answer B is wrong because the low pressure hose is connected to the low-side service valve.
Answer C is correct because when the system is completely empty, one connects the manifold gauge center hose to a vacuum pump.
Answer D is wrong because connecting the wrong hose to the vacuum pump can result in an inadequate evacuation.

Question #12
Answer A is wrong because the IAT sensor is a thermistor or negative temperature coefficient resistor, as the temperature increases the resistance decreases.
Answer B is wrong because the oxygen sensor generates a voltage.
Answer C is correct because the cab temperature sensor and a hot wire flow meter both use the principle of the Wheatstone bridge; i.e., a variable resistance resulting from changing pressures acting on a silicon disc. This action produces a voltage input to a control module.
Answer D is wrong because the TP sensor is a string sensor or variable resistor potentiometer. Pressure changes have no effect on this sensor.

Question #13
Answer A is correct because the Clean Air Act (CAA) established the rule of certification.
Answer B is wrong because this statement is in violation of the CAA.
Answer C is wrong because this statement is in violation of the CAA.
Answer D is wrong because this statement is in violation of the CAA.

Question #14
Answer A is wrong because restoration is a term generally applied to old buildings.
Answer B is wrong because recovery is the process by which refrigerant is removed from a system.
Answer C is correct because the recycling process reduces contaminants used in refrigerant by using oil separation and filter core driers.
Answer D is wrong because reclamation is an industrial process by which refrigerant is restored to its original condition.

Question #15
Answer A is wrong because the ATC control panel is not programmable.
Answer B is correct because you can often detect ATC system failures using a scan tool.
Answer C is wrong because only technician B is right.
Answer D is wrong because one of the technicians is right.

Question #16
Answer A is correct because the valve is front-seated when the stem is turned clockwise to seat the front valve face to the left, shutting off the flow of refrigerant to the compressor and isolating it.
Answer B is wrong because back seating the valve moves it clockwise to the right to seal the rear face valve. This is the normal valve position.
Answer C is wrong because when the valve is at mid-position, it is not seated at all.
Answer D is wrong because in normal operating position, the valve is back-seated.

Question #17
Answer A is a good choice because bubbles and or foam in the sight glass indicate the refrigerant charge is low and air has entered the system but it is wrong because both technicians are right.
Answer B is also a good choice because a cloudy sight glass indicates moisture in the system. However, the choice is wrong because both technicians are right.
Answer C is correct because both technicians are correct.
Answer D is wrong because both technicians are correct.

Question #18
Answer A is wrong because a bent mounting bracket can cause belt misalignment.
Answer B is wrong because a faulty clutch bearing can cause belt misalignment.
Answer C is correct because shimming the clutch plate sets the air gap and air gap will not affect belt alignment.
Answer D is wrong because a faulty idler pulley will cause belt misalignment.

Question #19
Answer A is wrong because the relationship of pressure to temperature at a constant volume is direct so that at 70°F the pressure is about 70 psi, not 220 psi.
Answer B is wrong because the relationship of pressure to temperature at a constant volume is direct so that at 70°F the pressure is about 70 psi, not 125 psi.
Answer C is correct because the relationship of pressure to temperature at a constant volume is direct so that at 70°F the pressure is about 70 psi. This is known as Charles Gas Law.
Answer D is wrong because the relationship of pressure to temperature at a constant volume is direct so that at 70°F the pressure is about 70 psi, not 30 psi.

Question #20
Answer A is wrong because the reaction plate is red.
Answer B is wrong because a yellow or green flame indicates a small leak.
Answer C is wrong because the flame is normally pale blue.
Answer D is correct because in the presence of a large leak, the flame will be purple.

Question #21
Answer A is wrong because the heater control valves are not operated by engine speed.
Answer B is correct because the heater control valves may be cable operated or vacuum operated.
Answer C is wrong because only technician B is correct.
Answer D is wrong because one of the technicians is right.

Question #22
Answer A is wrong because when the pressure bleeds down at all, the heater core is leaking and must be replaced.
Answer B is wrong because if the heater core leaks, it should be replaced immediately to prevent coolant loss and the risk of engine damage.
Answer C is correct because when you test a heater core for leaks, you apply 10 psi of air pressure and the pressure bleeds to 5 psi in 3 minutes.
Answer D is wrong because this is an acceptable method of checking a heater core for leaks.

Question #23
Answer A is correct because this is an acceptable method of repairing a stripped mounting bolt-hole.
Answer B is wrong because the compressor can be repaired.
Answer C is wrong because only one of the technicians is right.
Answer D is wrong because only one of the technicians is right.

Question #24
Answer A is wrong because raising the pressure of the cooling system raises the boiling point of the coolant.
Answer B is correct because raising the pressure compresses the rate of gas expansion, thereby increasing the temperature to reach the boiling point.
Answer C is wrong because raising the pressure in the cooling system does not prevent corrosion.
Answer D is wrong because raising the pressure does affect boiling point.

Question #25
Answer A is wrong because you cannot adjust an expansion valve with any process.
Answer B is wrong because you cannot adjust an expansion valve with any process.
Answer C is wrong because you cannot adjust an expansion valve with any process.
Answer D is correct because you cannot adjust the expansion valve.

Question #26
Answer A is wrong because shutoff valves must be located within 12 inches of the ends of the hoses.
Answer B is correct because new environmental laws dictate that shutoff valves must be located no more than 12 inches from test hose service end.
Answer C is wrong because one of the technicians is right.
Answer D is wrong because one of the technicians is right.

Question #27
Answer A is correct because PAG oil is specifically formulated to be compatible with R-134a.
Answer B is wrong because R-12 systems use mineral based lubricant.
Answer C is wrong because DEXRON is not compatible with R-134a and will damage A/C system components.
Answer D is wrong because SAE 30 you place the sensor probe just below the fitting and will damage A/C system components.

Question #28
Answer A is correct because a broken blend door cable will make HVAC output temperature uncontrollable.
Answer B is wrong because a defective compressor clutch will not affect heater temperature control.
Answer C is wrong because a clogged orifice tube will not affect heater temperature control.
Answer D is wrong because an inoperative blower motor has no affect on temperature control.

Question #29
Answer A is wrong because many ATC systems use a sun sensor to gauge the intensity of the sunlight entering the vehicle.
Answer B is wrong because virtually all ATC systems use an ambient temperature sensor.
Answer C is wrong because an evaporator temperature sensor is used to tell the controller when to disengage the compressor.
Answer D is correct because the manifold pressure sensor is an input to the diesel electronic fuel injection control unit.

Question #30
Answer A is a good choice but wrong because excessive high-side pressure that caused the pressure relief valve on the A/C compressor to operate might have been the result of a faulty engine cooling fan clutch. A faulty shutter control valve could also cause the pressure relief valve to operate.
Answer B is also a good choice but wrong because the relief valve might have operated due to a faulty shutter control solenoid. An inoperative fan clutch could also cause the pressure relief valve to operate.
Answer C is correct because both technicians are right.
Answer D is wrong because both technicians are correct.

Question #31
Answer A is correct because if the air gap is too great the clutch will slip.
Answer B is wrong because the drive and driven plates must be replaced.
Answer C is wrong because only one technician is right.
Answer D is wrong because one of the technicians is right.

Question #32
Answer A is wrong because this is not an acceptable method of adjusting the lubricant level in the system.
Answer B is wrong because this is not an acceptable method of adjusting the lubricant level in the system.
Answer C is correct because the only accurate way to measure the amount of oil in a compressor is to remove it and measure.
Answer D is wrong because this method will result in overfilling the compressor.

Question #33
Answer A is wrong because oil must be added to the evaporator prior to installation.
Answer B is wrong because oil must be added to the condenser prior to installation.
Answer C is wrong because oil must be added to the accumulator prior to installation.
Answer D is correct because the addition of refrigerant oil is not required when replacing the suction throttling valve.

Question #34
Answer A is wrong because debris trapped in the condenser fins will significantly affect air flow through the condenser.
Answer B is correct because relative humidity will not significantly affect air flow through the condenser.
Answer C is wrong because bent fins will affect air flow through the condenser.
Answer D is wrong because vehicle speed will affect air flow through the condenser.

Question #35
Answer A is wrong because damaged or misaligned condenser mounts can cause condenser or refrigerant line damage due to abrasion or fatigue.
Answer B is correct because deformed or improperly aligned condenser mounting insulators could damage the condenser and refrigerant lines.
Answer C is wrong because only one technician is right.
Answer D is wrong because one of the technicians is right.

Question #36
Answer A is correct because if the A/C system is open for an extended period of time, the desiccant in the receiver/drier will become saturated with moisture and must be replaced.
Answer B is wrong because the receiver/drier only needs to be replaced if it is damaged or if the desiccant bag is saturated or damaged.
Answer C is wrong because there is no mileage requirement for replacement of the receiver/drier.
Answer D is wrong because compressor replacement does not necessitate receiver/drier replacement.

Question #37
Answer A is wrong because the evaporator drain is the most likely place to detect refrigerant leaking from the evaporator core.
Answer B is correct because the expansion valve is outside the evaporator case.
Answer C is wrong because refrigerant leaking from the evaporator core can often be detected at the panel vents.
Answer D is wrong because refrigerant leaking from the evaporator core can often be detected at the panel vents.

Question #38
Answer A is correct because vinegar will kill the mold and mildew that is the source of the odor.
Answer B is wrong because this method will simply mask the odor and not eliminate the problem.
Answer C is wrong because this method poses a possible fire hazard.
Answer D is wrong because this method will simply mask the odor and not eliminate the problem.

Question #39
Answer A is correct because the Schrader valve has a removable core.
Answer B is wrong because Schrader service valves do not provide a means to the front seat or rear seat valve.
Answer C is wrong because only technician A is correct.
Answer D is wrong because one of the technicians is right.

Question #40
Answer A is correct because any leak from the system must be repaired as quickly as possible.
Answer B is wrong because if oil is leaking from the system, refrigerant is also leaking from the system.
Answer C is wrong because only technician A is correct.
Answer D is wrong because one of the technicians is correct.

Question #41
Answer A is wrong because a clogged evaporator drain will cause fogging on the inside of the windshield.
Answer B is wrong because a leaking heater core will cause fogging on the inside of the heater core.
Answer C is wrong because an iced-up evaporator core will not cause the windshield to fog.
Answer D is correct because under these conditions a cold windshield causes moisture to condense from the outside air.

Question #42
Answer A is correct because the hydrometer measures the specific gravity of the coolant relative to that of known good coolant.
Answer B is wrong because a spectrophotometer is an expensive piece of laboratory apparatus that calculates the concentration of particulate in a fluid.
Answer C is wrong because using a balance scale to determine the protection level of coolant is labor intensive.
Answer D is wrong because color is not always a good measure of protection level.

Question #43
Answer A is wrong because a bulge in the hose indicates a weak spot.
Answer B is correct because the hose should be replaced immediately.
Answer C is wrong because only one technician is right.
Answer D is wrong because one technician is right.

Question #44
Answer A is correct because a growling noise from the water pump indicates a worn bearing.
Answer B is wrong because cavitation damage will not cause this symptom.
Answer C is wrong because only one technician is right.
Answer D is wrong because one technician is right.

Question #45
Answer A is wrong because when the thermostat opens, the upper radiator hose rapidly gets warm.
Answer B is wrong because when the thermostat opens, the temperature gauge rises until it indicates normal operating temperature.
Answer C is wrong because when the thermostat is open, there is obvious circulation motion in the upper radiator tank.
Answer D is correct because thermostat opening is often not noticeable in the surge tank.

Question #46
Answer A is correct because when you increase the radiator pressure, you increase the boiling point, not decrease it.
Answer B is wrong because it is true when more antifreeze is added to the coolant mix, the boiling point is increased.
Answer C is wrong because it is true that good quality ethylene glycol antifreeze contains a corrosion inhibitor.
Answer D is wrong because it is true that coolant solutions must be recovered, recycled, or handled as hazardous material.

Question #47
Answer A is correct because replacing the coolant conditioner cartridge is an important part of regular engine maintenance.
Answer B is wrong because the coolant conditioner must be changed regularly.
Answer C is wrong because only one technician is right.
Answer D is wrong because one technician is right.

Question #48
Answer A is wrong because you replace a cracked fan blade, not weld it.
Answer B is wrong because you do not repair a cracked fan blade.
Answer C is wrong because neither technician is right.
Answer D is correct because both technicians are wrong.

Question #49
Answer A is wrong because the coolant level must be lowered only to a height below the valve.
Answer B is correct you do not have to drain the entire system.
Answer C is wrong because the cable needs to be replaced only if it is damaged.
Answer D is wrong because the system must be bled after the repair is complete.

Question #50
Answer A is wrong because shutters stuck open will not cause the engine to overheat.
Answer B is wrong because shutters stuck open will not cause excessive high-side pressure.
Answer C is wrong because the air pressure relief valve can still operate with the shutters stuck open.
Answer D is correct because if the shutters are stuck open, the engine will warm up slowly.

Question #51

Answer A is a good choice because the binary pressure switch prevents compressor operation if the refrigerant charge has been lost or ambient temperature too cold. The binary switch also protects the system from excessive pressure.

Answer B is also a good choice because the binary pressure switch turns off the compressor if the system pressure is too high. The binary switch also protects the system from low-pressure operation.

Answer C is correct because both technicians are right.

Answer D is wrong because neither technician is wrong.

Question #52

Answer A is correct because if the coolant temperature rises to a predetermined level, the PCM will disengage the compressor clutch.

Answer B is wrong because the IAT sensor signal is not used to control compressor operation.

Answer C is wrong because the oxygen sensor signal is not used to control compressor operation.

Answer D is wrong because there is no cooling fan sensor.

Question #53

Answer A is wrong because electric cooling fans are often controlled by an electronic relay.

Answer B is wrong because a cooling fan module often controls electric cooling fans.

Answer C is wrong because a multiplexed electronic module often controls electric cooling fans.

Answer D is correct because there is no air solenoid controller.

Question #54

Answer A is wrong because you do not mount the door using an adhesive.

Answer B is wrong because you do not mount the door using an adhesive.

Answer C is wrong because the location varies with the truck.

Answer D is correct because the blend door actuator is generally mounted to the evaporator case.

Question #55

Answer A is wrong because a blown fuse or other faults could cause the problem.

Answer B is wrong because feedback could not cause this symptom.

Answer C is wrong because both technicians are wrong.

Answer D is correct because neither technician is correct.

Question #56

Answer A is wrong because to avoid repeat repairs, the temperature control lever should not be repaired, only replaced.

Answer B is correct because you should replace the control head.

Answer C is wrong because only technician B is right.

Answer D is wrong because one technician is right.

Question #57

Answer A is wrong because applying shop air to a vacuum actuator will damage the actuator.

Answer B is correct because if the actuator holds vacuum, the diaphragm is OK.

Answer C is wrong because testing an actuator in this manner could condemn a good component.

Answer D is wrong because the evacuation pump is an appropriate tool to test actuators.

Question #58

Answer A is wrong because many HVAC systems do not use vacuum at all.

Answer B is wrong because this describes the purpose of a vacuum delay valve.

Answer C is wrong because vacuum actuators are not damaged by sudden changes in vacuum.

Answer D is correct because a vacuum check valve prevents loss of vacuum to components during periods of low engine vacuum.

Question #59
Answer A is wrong because it is important to keep water drained from the system to reduce internal corrosion.
Answer B is wrong because some fan clutches are operated using chassis air.
Answer C is wrong because most radiator shutter systems are air-operated.
Answer D is correct because no accessory is integral with the chassis air system because they are separated by a pressure protection valve to prevent air loss top the brakes.

Question #60
Answer A is correct because a misaligned duct could cause a whistling noise.
Answer B is wrong because a defective actuator will not cause this symptom.
Answer C is wrong because an improperly adjusted cable will not cause this symptom.
Answer D is wrong because a poor connection will not cause this symptom.

Question #61
Answer A is wrong because a defective control module will not prevent the blend door from moving.
Answer B is wrong because a defective feedback device will not prevent the door from moving when the motor runs.
Answer C is correct because a defective drive gear in the actuator will cause this condition.
Answer D is wrong because an improperly adjusted ATC sensor cable will not cause this condition.

Question #62
Answer A is wrong because chassis air pressure can be used to operate a coolant control valve.
Answer B is wrong because vacuum can be used to operate a coolant control valve.
Answer C is wrong because early ATC systems used a cable to operate the coolant control valve.
Answer D is correct because a magneto is used to generate the ignition spark in many small gasoline engines.

Question #63
Answer A is correct because a 12-volt test light is a valuable tool for diagnosing electric actuators and solenoids.
Answer B is wrong because a self-powered test light is used to check circuit continuity.
Answer C is wrong because a hand-held scan tool is more valuable for diagnosing electronic components.
Answer D is wrong because a charging station is used to add refrigerant to the A/C system.

Question #64
Answer A is correct because the control panel should be replaced when one segment of the digital read-out on an ATC control panel is inoperative
Answer B is wrong because LED's cannot be replaced in the field.
Answer C is wrong because only one technician is right.
Answer D is wrong because one technician is right.

Question #65
Answer A is wrong because ATC system calibration is usually checked with a thermometer.
Answer B is wrong because ATC system calibration is not usually adjustable in the field.
Answer C is wrong because both technicians are wrong.
Answer D is correct because neither technician is right.

Question #66
Answer A is wrong because you can install refrigerant through both service valves when the engine is not running.
Answer B is wrong because one can install refrigerant through the low-side service valve when the engine is running.
Answer C is correct because you never attempt to charge an A/C system through the high-side service valve when the engine is running because compressor damage will result.
Answer D is wrong because one may charge an A/C systems directly from an approved charging station.

Question #67
Answer A is wrong because a faulty compressor discharge valve will not cause a band of frost on the high-pressure hose.
Answer B is correct because a restriction in the high-pressure hose can cause a band of frost on the high-pressure hose.
Answer C is wrong because a clogged orifice tube will not cause a band of frost on the high-pressure hose.
Answer D is wrong because moisture in the system will not cause a band of frost on the high-pressure hose.

Question #68
Answer A is correct because each of these devices has a variable orifice to regulate the pressure, and thereby the temperature in the evaporator.
Answer B is wrong because the purpose of these devices is to control evaporator pressure.
Answer C is wrong because "compressor pressure" is an ambiguous term.
Answer D is wrong because liquid line pressure is the same as condenser pressure.

Question #69
Answer A is wrong because petroleum jelly must not be used to lubricate O-rings.
Answer B is wrong because transmission fluid can damage A/C O-rings.
Answer C is wrong because silicone grease must not be introduced into the system.
Answer D is correct because refrigeration oil is the only acceptable lubricant for A/C O-rings.

Question #70
Answer A is correct because most HVAC control panels contain independent switch modules.
Answer B is wrong because most truck control panel components are serviceable.
Answer C is wrong because only technician A is right.
Answer D is wrong because one of the technicians is right.

Question #71
Answer A is correct because the engine cooling fan is usually controlled mechanically or by the engine control module.
Answer B is wrong because the ATC system controls the blower motor.
Answer C is wrong because the ATC system controls the blend door actuator to modulate the output air temperature.
Answer D is wrong because the ATC system controls the position of the outside air door.

Answers to the Test Questions for the Additional Test Questions Section 6

1.	C	34.	C	67.	B	100.	D
2.	A	35.	C	68.	A	101.	A
3.	B	36.	D	69.	D	102.	B
4.	C	37.	D	70.	C	103.	A
5.	B	38.	C	71.	D	104.	A
6.	D	39.	C	72.	C	105.	D
7.	C	40.	C	73.	B	106.	D
8.	A	41.	C	74.	B	107.	D
9.	D	42.	D	75.	D	108.	D
10.	B	43.	B	76.	A	109.	C
11.	A	44.	D	77.	C	110.	B
12.	A	45.	A	78.	D	111.	B
13.	A	46.	D	79.	B	112.	D
14.	A	47.	B	80.	A	113.	B
15.	D	48.	D	81.	A	114.	D
16.	D	49.	C	82.	D	115.	D
17.	B	50.	B	83.	C	116.	A
18.	A	51.	A	84.	B	117.	A
19.	C	52.	B	85.	C	118.	B
20.	C	53.	B	86.	D	119.	A
21.	A	54.	C	87.	B	120.	A
22.	D	55.	B	88.	C	121.	D
23.	C	56.	C	89.	B	122.	C
24.	B	57.	A	90.	C	123.	D
25.	B	58.	A	91.	C	124.	C
26.	B	59.	B	92.	A	125.	D
27.	B	60.	D	93.	B	126.	B
28.	C	61.	A	94.	A	127.	B
29.	C	62.	D	95.	B	128.	B
30.	B	63.	B	96.	B	129.	A
31.	A	64.	A	97.	D	130.	C
32.	D	65.	C	98.	B	131.	D
33.	A	66.	A	99.	D	132.	A

133.	A	141.	C	149.	C	157.	D
134.	C	142.	B	150.	B	158.	B
135.	A	143.	C	151.	B	159.	A
136.	B	144.	C	152.	C	160.	B
137.	A	145.	C	153.	B	161.	A
138.	B	146.	B	154.	A	162.	C
139.	D	147.	C	155.	A	163.	B
140.	D	148.	B	156.	C		

Explanations to the Answers for the Additional Test Questions Section 6

Question #1
Answer A is wrong because an improperly adjusted coolant control valve cable could also cause insufficient heater output.
Answer B is wrong because a clogged heater core could also cause insufficient heater output.
Answer C is correct because both technicians are right.
Answer D is wrong because both technicians are right.

Question #2
Answer A is correct because if the fan clutch is always engaged, it will enhance the operation of the A/C system.
Answer B is wrong because an improperly adjusted blend door cable will cause poor A/C performance.
Answer C is wrong because a low refrigerant charge will cause poor A/C system performance.
Answer D is wrong because a refrigerant overcharge will cause poor A/C system performance.

Question #3
Answer A is wrong because the back-seated position is the normal operating position.
Answer B is correct because with the service valve in the front-seated position, compressor damage will result.
Answer C is wrong because the mid-position is used when a manifold gauge set is hooked up.
Answer D is wrong because the high-side service valve is typically hot when the compressor is running.

Question #4
Answer A is wrong because fan clutch replacement does not affect the life of the water pump.
Answer B is wrong because the water pump generally has a longer service life than the heater hoses.
Answer C is correct because even a small leak from the weep hole indicates that the front seal of the water pump has failed.
Answer D is wrong because thermostat operation does not indicate a need to replace the water pump.

Question #5
Answer A is wrong because any acids that form in the A/C system are created due to moisture and corrosion and are usually in a liquid state.
Answer B is correct because air is not condensable at A/C system pressures.
Answer C is wrong because moisture in the A/C system only evaporates when the system is drawn under a vacuum, and is therefore normally in a liquid state.
Answer D is wrong because refrigeration oil is normally in a liquid state.

Question #6
Answer A is wrong because the thermostat will not fit into the housing.
Answer B is wrong because it will not fit in that direction.
Answer C is wrong because the thermostat is not installed in the proximity of the core.
Answer D is correct because the spring controls the valve in the thermostat, opening when it gets to the desired operating temperature. Since the engine block is the source of heat, the spring must face the engine block.

Question #7
Answer A is wrong because you cannot sense evaporator temperature inside car temperature from the engine compartment, where the condenser is located.
Answer B is wrong because you use an accumulator with a CCOT system that does use a thermal bulb or capillary tube.
Answer C is correct because the thermal bulb and capillary tube are part of the thermal expansion valve located near the evaporator.
Answer D is wrong because a CCOT system does use a thermal bulb or capillary tube.

Question #8
Answer A is correct because a cloudy sight glass indicates that the desiccant bag in the receiver/drier has broken.
Answer B is wrong because the receiver/drier must be replaced if the desiccant bag breaks down or if the system has been open for an extended period of time.
Answer C is wrong because only one technician is right.
Answer D is wrong because one of the technicians is right.

Question #9
Answer A is wrong because a leaking heater core will cause windshield fogging in the DEFROST mode.
Answer B is wrong because a clogged evaporator drain will cause windshield fogging in the DEFROST mode.
Answer C is wrong because an exterior water leak into the air intake plenum can cause windshield fogging in the DEFROST mode.
Answer D is correct because moisture in the refrigerant will not cause windshield fogging.

Question #10
Answer A is wrong because a clogged evaporator drain will not cause a whistling noise.
Answer B is correct because a cracked evaporator case could cause a whistling noise.
Answer C is wrong because a broken blend door cable will not cause a whistling noise.
Answer D is wrong because a low refrigerant charge will not cause a whistling noise.

Question #11
Answer A is correct because this is the proper method of checking the oil level in the compressor.
Answer B is wrong because simply adding an oil charge could result in too much lubricant in the system.
Answer C is wrong because only technician A is right.
Answer D is wrong because one of the technicians is right.

Question #12
Answer A is correct because antifreeze raises the boiling point of the coolant, not the conditioner.
Answer B is wrong because the coolant conditioner cartridge filters particulate from the coolant.
Answer C is wrong because the coolant conditioner internally lubricates the cooling system.
Answer D is wrong because the coolant conditioner prevents cavitation corrosion of the cylinder liners.

Question #13
Answer A is correct because using a belt tension gauge ensures that the belt is properly adjusted.
Answer B is wrong because this method does not ensure proper belt tension.
Answer C is wrong because this method does not ensure proper belt tension.
Answer D is wrong because this method could cause engine damage due to overtightening.

Question #14
Answer A is correct because the high pressure refrigerant at the compressor outlet can raise the temperature of the outlet to that of the engine coolant.
Answer B is wrong because this is a normal condition.
Answer C is wrong because only one of the technicians is right.
Answer D is wrong because one of the technicians is right.

Question #15
Answer A is wrong because to prevent damaging A/C system components, the nitrogen pressure must be regulated.
Answer B is wrong because the A/C compressor must be disconnected before flushing the system.
Answer C is wrong because to avoid damaging restrictive components, they must be removed before flushing.
Answer D is correct because one can vent nitrogen to the atmosphere.

Question #16
Answer A is wrong because improper radiator shutter operation can cause the relief valve to operate.
Answer B is wrong because a clogged condenser will cause the relief valve to operate.
Answer C is wrong because an inoperative fan clutch will cause the relief valve to operate.
Answer D is correct because a defective A/C compressor will not cause the relief valve to operate.

Question #17
Answer A is wrong because a cracked mounting plate could cause drive belt wear.
Answer B is correct because a cracked mounting plate will not cause internal compressor damage.
Answer C is wrong because a cracked mounting plate can cause a vibration with the compressor clutch engaged.
Answer D is wrong because a cracked mounting plate can cause belt squeal or chatter.

Question #18
Answer A is correct because comparing the pressure of recovered refrigerant to the theoretical pressure of pure refrigerant at a given temperature is the best method of testing for non-condensable gases in refrigerant.
Answer B is wrong because pressure cannot be compared to humidity.
Answer C is wrong because pressure cannot be compared to volume.
Answer D is wrong because a halogen leak detector cannot be used to check for non- condensable gases.

Question #19
Answer A is wrong because a spring lock tool is the tool shown.
Answer B is wrong because a bearing puller is not shown.
Answer C is correct because this is the tool shown in the figure.
Answer D is wrong because a flare tool is not shown.

Question #20
Answer A is wrong because recycled refrigerant must also contain less then 330 ppm of non-condensable gases.
Answer B is wrong because recycled refrigerant must also contain less than 15 ppm of moisture.
Answer C is correct because both technicians are right.
Answer D is wrong because neither technician is wrong.

Question #21
Answer A is correct because a digital multimeter (DMM) is the most precise tool for electrical/electronic components or systems and because of its 10 Megohm impedance, it will not harm solid-state components.
Answer B is wrong because a self-powered test lamp could damage solid-state components.
Answer C is wrong because an analog VOM can damage solid-state components.
Answer D is wrong because a 12V test lamp can damage solid-state components.

Question #22
Answer A is wrong because this temperature is too low.
Answer B is wrong because this temperature is too low.
Answer C is wrong because this temperature is still too low.
Answer D is correct because blower operation is delayed to prevent air from entering the cab at an uncomfortable temperature.

Question #23
Answer A is a good choice because most ATC systems have some type of internal diagnostic routine. You can also display DTCs on the control panel or a scan tool.
Answer B is good choice because you can also display DTCs on the control panel or a scan tool. Most ATC systems have some type of internal diagnostic routine.
Answer C is correct because both technicians are right.
Answer D is wrong because neither technician is wrong.

Question #24
Answer A is wrong because refrigerant oil must be added to the evaporator prior to installation.
Answer B is correct because most manufacturers recommend that 3 ounces of oil be added to a new evaporator.
Answer C is wrong because nine ounces of refrigerant oil would cause an excessive system oil level.
Answer D is wrong because the entire A/C system is likely to contain about fourteen and a half ounces of oil.

Question #25
Answer A is wrong because some coolant control valves close when vacuum is removed.
Answer B is correct because this process allows the technician to check the specific coolant flow valve operation.
Answer C is wrong because only one of the technicians is right.
Answer D is wrong because one of the technicians is right.

Question #26
Answer A is wrong because to directly test a thermostat, it must be removed from the vehicle.
Answer B is correct because a technician uses a pressure tester to test radiators, pressure caps, and hoses for leaks.
Answer C is wrong because A/C leaks must be located using a leak detector.
Answer D is wrong because vacuum diaphragms are tested using a hand-held vacuum pump.

Question #27
Answer A is wrong because current to run the blower at low speed must pass through the resistor for medium speed as well.
Answer B is correct because the switch provides the path for current to the medium speed resistor.
Answer C is wrong because only one technician is correct.
Answer D is wrong because one technician is correct.

Question #28
Answer A is wrong because a black light is only useful when a special dye is introduced into the cooling system.
Answer B is wrong because a leak detector is used to find refrigerant leaks.
Answer C is correct because a good visual inspection will locate any coolant leaks.
Answer D is wrong because white smoke is evidence of burning antifreeze.

Question #29
Answer A is wrong because grit in the evaporator case is not likely to cause this symptom.
Answer B is wrong because the mode door does not move when the temperature setting is changed.
Answer C is correct because bad drive gears in the blend door motor will cause this symptom.
Answer D is wrong because arcing in the control head will not cause a grinding noise.

Question #30
Answer A is wrong because the shape of a preformed hose is derived during the manufacturing process.
Answer B is correct because the spring provides internal support.
Answer C is wrong because the resilience of the hose comes from the rubber.
Answer D is wrong because the strength of the hose comes from the fibers inside.

Question #31
Answer A is correct because A/C fittings should not be disturbed if they are not leaking.
Answer B is wrong because an A/C maintenance service should include cleaning the condenser fins.
Answer C is wrong because an A/C maintenance service should include straightening bent condenser fins.
Answer D is wrong because an A/C maintenance service should include checking all component mounts and insulators.

Question #32
Answer A is wrong because flushing the cooling system removes rust from the system.
Answer B is wrong because flushing the cooling system removes contaminants from the system.
Answer C is wrong because flushing the cooling system can increase the life of the system components.
Answer D is correct because acids of combustion are found in the engine oil, not in the coolant.

Question #33
Answer A is correct because the expansion valve is located at the evaporator inlet.
Answer B is wrong because this is the wrong location.
Answer C is wrong because this is the wrong location.
Answer D is wrong because this is the wrong location.

Question #34
Answer A is wrong because the heater core does not need insulation.
Answer B is wrong because the heater core does not contribute significantly to cab noise.
Answer C is correct because foam tape can be used to cushion and seal around the heater core.
Answer D is wrong because a gasket is provided to seal around heater hose connections.

Question #35
Answer A is a good choice because the tanks are color-coded. However, A is wrong because both technicians are right.
Answer B is also a good choice because the fitting is also a 1/2 inch, ACME. However, B is wrong because both technicians are right.
Answer C is correct because both technicians are right.
Answer D is wrong because both technicians are right.

Question #36
Answer A is wrong because the antifreeze and water can be added in any order.
Answer B is wrong because the antifreeze and water can be added in any order.
Answer C is wrong because there is no need to premix the coolant.
Answer D is correct because it is important to bleed the system.

Question #37
Answer A is wrong because some fan clutches are air operated.
Answer B is wrong because some fan clutches are operated by a thermostatic spring.
Answer C is wrong because some fans use a viscous clutch.
Answer D is correct because hydraulic switches are rarely used.

Question #38
Answer A is wrong because applying power and ground to the appropriate terminals can also test the coil.
Answer B is wrong because the coil can also be tested with an ohmmeter.
Answer C is correct because both technicians are right.
Answer D is wrong because neither technician is wrong.

Question #39
Answer A is a good choice because all electronic HVAC actuators use some type of feedback device. However, A is wrong because both technicians are right.
Answer B is is also a good choice because all electronic HVAC actuators use some sort of feedback device. However, B is wrong because both technicians are right.
Answer C is correct because both technicians are right.
Answer D is wrong because both technicians are right.

Question #40
Answer A is a good choice but wrong, because it is also important to use only the correct type and amount of oil.
Answer B is a good choice but wrong, because the oil needs to be checked if there has been a significant loss of oil.
Answer C is correct because both technicians are right.
Answer D is wrong because both technicians are right.

Question #41
Answer A is a good choice but wrong, because most trucks are also equipped with an override switch.
Answer B is also a good choice but wrong, because many trucks are also equipped with a shutdown alarm.
Answer C is correct because both technicians are right.
Answer D is wrong because neither technician is wrong.

Question #42
Answer A is wrong because a defective blower switch could prevent clutch engagement by not allowing current to flow from the white wire to the mode control switch.
Answer B is wrong because an open binary pressure control switch will prevent clutch engagement because it is in the path.
Answer C is wrong because a poor connection at the thermostat switch could prevent clutch engagement.
Answer D is correct because if this fuse opens it only affects the panel light and will not prevent clutch engagement.

Question #43
Answer A is wrong because the purchaser is under no legal obligation to maintain records.
Answer B is correct because refrigerant suppliers must maintain records about all facilities to which refrigerant is sent.
Answer C is wrong because only one technician is right.
Answer D is wrong because one technician is right.

Question #44
Answer A is wrong because the high-pressure relief valve resets itself when system pressures return to normal.
Answer B is wrong because the high-pressure relief valve is individually replaceable.
Answer C is wrong because both technicians are wrong.
Answer D is correct because neither technician is right.

Question #45
Answer A is correct because most shutter systems are air operated, not electrically operated.
Answer B is wrong because an air leak could cause the shutters to remain open.
Answer C is wrong because dirt accumulation on the shutter linkage could prevent the shutters from closing completely.
Answer D is wrong because ice build-up could prevent the shutters from closing completely.

Question #46
Answer A is wrong because using an ohmmeter will typically not provide calibration.
Answer B is wrong because this process only checks that sensor.
Answer C is wrong because not all ATC units have such a dial.
Answer D is correct because the easiest way to check the calibration of an ATC system is to measure the cab temperature using a thermometer.

Question #47
Answer A is wrong because the replacement of cables with small airlines simplifies control panel replacement.
Answer B is correct because coolant control valves are sometimes operated by chassis air.
Answer C is wrong because in air controlled HVAC systems, the mode and blend air cylinders typically operate air doors.
Answer D is wrong because air leaks can cause mode and blend air doors to react sluggishly or to be inoperative.

Question #48
Answer A is wrong because a binding door will not cause the actuator to hunt for the proper position.
Answer B is wrong because a faulty motor will not cause the actuator to hunt for the desired position.
Answer C is wrong because an improperly adjusted cable will not cause the actuator to hunt for the desired position.
Answer D is correct because a faulty feedback device can cause the blend air door to hunt for the desired position.

Question #49
Answer A is wrong because the engine must not be running when an air line is being removed from the vehicle.
Answer B is wrong because there is no need to drain water from the system before replacing a hose.
Answer C is correct because you drain all air from the system before attempting to replace any chassis air component.
Answer D is wrong because there is no need to remove the compressor from the vehicle when replacing an air hose.

Question #50
Answer A is wrong because most ATCs connect to the engine fuel management system.
Answer B is correct because most of these systems connect closely to the engine control system.
Answer C is wrong because only one of the technicians is right.
Answer D is wrong one of the technicians is right.

Question #51
Answer A is correct because R-134a has a faint ether-like odor.
Answer B is wrong because R-12 is odorless.
Answer C is wrong because HVAC system input air is not drawn from under the hood or the cab.
Answer D is wrong because a leaking heater core will not produce an ether-like odor.

Question #52
Answer A is wrong because a cracked or bent mounting bracket can cause drive belt edge wear.
Answer B is correct because compressor clutch air gap does not affect pulley alignment.
Answer C is wrong because a damaged compressor pulley could cause drive belt edge wear.
Answer D is wrong because a worn idler pulley bearing could cause belt misalignment and result in edge wear.

Question #53
Answer A is wrong because the condenser should not be replaced, rather it should be cleaned.
Answer B is correct because several bent fins and a moderate accumulation of dead insects will not restrict air flow through the condenser enough to cause the high-pressure relief valve to operate.
Answer C is wrong because only one technician is right.
Answer D is wrong because one technician is right.

Question #54
Answer A is wrong because a vacuum check valve does not delay the passage of vacuum to components.
Answer B is wrong because a check valve does not switch vacuum on or off.
Answer C is correct because it prevents a vacuum drop during periods of low source vacuum.
Answer D is wrong because a vacuum check valve is not a sensor.

Question #55
Answer A is wrong because 3 psi is far too low.
Answer B is correct because heavy-duty truck cooling systems are typically pressurized to about 10 psi to 15 psi.
Answer C is wrong because 20 psi is too high.
Answer D is wrong because 30 psi is very high.

Question #56
Answer A is wrong because the blend door actuator should not bleed vacuum.
Answer B is wrong because a vacuum operated actuator does not contain a motor.
Answer C is correct because a vacuum actuator door should hold vacuum indefinitely.
Answer D is wrong because the vacuum actuator diaphragm is not porous.

Question #57
Answer A is correct because the best way to repair wiring is by soldering.
Answer B is wrong because twisting wires together and taping them will result in a high resistance connection and ultimately circuit failure.
Answer C is wrong because only one technician is right.
Answer D is wrong because one technician is right.

Question #58
Answer A is correct because replacement is the only good repair for an HVAC control panel with an air leak.
Answer B is wrong because this process will not work.
Answer C is wrong because this process will not work.
Answer D is wrong because this process will not work.

Question #59
Answer A is wrong because it does not provide a boosting function.
Answer B is correct because the A/C high pressure switch opens the electrical circuit to the compressor clutch coil when high-side pressure reaches its upper limit.
Answer C is wrong because it does not maintain pressure.
Answer D is wrong because it does perform a venting function.

Question #60
Answer A is wrong because some evaporator filters are made of paper or a metallic mesh.
Answer B is wrong because evaporator filters are not designed to remove moisture from the air.
Answer C is wrong because evaporator filters are replaceable.
Answer D is correct because they are designed to remove dust and dirt from cab and sleeper air.

Question #61
Answer A is correct because a misaligned air duct could cause inadequate air flow from one or more vents.
Answer B is wrong because a faulty blower resistor will affect air flow from all vents in one or more blower speed settings.
Answer C is wrong because a clogged heater core will not affect output air flow.
Answer D is wrong because high humidity will not affect output air flow.

Question #62
Answer A is wrong because the fan blade will freewheel at a reduced speed due to friction/viscous forces.
Answer B is wrong because the engine idle will rise slightly or be unaffected.
Answer C is wrong because the shutters may or may not be closed.
Answer D is correct because the fan blade may freewheel at a reduced speed.

Question #63
Answer A is wrong because a defective unloader can cause the compressor to build up excessive system pressure.
Answer B is correct because a defective moisture drain will not cause the relief valve to operate.
Answer C is wrong because a weak spring in the regulator will cause the relief valve to operate at a lower than normal pressure.
Answer D is wrong because a defective governor could cause this problem.

Question #64
Answer A is correct because the shutter cylinder must be replaced.
Answer B is wrong because shutter cylinders cannot be overhauled.
Answer C is wrong because only technician A is right.
Answer D is wrong because one technician is right.

Question #65
Answer A is wrong because a faulty thermostat can cause poor coolant circulation.
Answer B is wrong because an eroded water pump impeller will cause poor coolant circulation.
Answer C is correct because the upper hose is under pressure and is unlikely to collapse.
Answer D is wrong because the lower hose carries coolant to the intake side of the water pump and could collapse.

Question #66
Answer A is correct because this symptom is typical of an A/C system with an evaporator icing problem, which could be caused by a defective thermal expansion valve.
Answer B is wrong because a defective coolant control valve would not cause the A/C system output air to change from cold to warm.
Answer C is wrong because the blend air door does not typically have a return spring.
Answer D is wrong because the fresh air door does not control the output air temperature.

Question #67
Answer A is wrong because the switch is not necessarily at fault.
Answer B is correct because low refrigerant charge will cause this symptom.
Answer C is wrong because only one technician is right.
Answer D is wrong because one technician is right.

Question #68
Answer A is correct because the condenser generally holds 1 ounce of refrigeration oil.
Answer B is wrong because this amount is too large.
Answer C is wrong because this amount is too large.
Answer D is wrong because this amount is too large.

Question #69
Answer A is wrong because the evaporator is not a cooling system component.
Answer B is wrong because the power steering cooler is not a cooling system component.
Answer C is wrong because the oil cooler is not a cooling system component.
Answer D is correct because a blown head gasket is the most likely cause of an internal engine coolant leak.

Question #70
Answer A is wrong because battery removal has no effect on this service.
Answer B is wrong because this has no bearing on the removal process.
Answer C is correct because if the blend air door is binding, it could damage the new actuator.
Answer D is wrong because this is not a sensitive CMOS electronic component.

Question #71
Answer A is wrong because a vacuum leak will cause inoperative HVAC mode switch.
Answer B is wrong because an air leak will cause inoperative HVAC mode switch.
Answer C is wrong because a broken cable will cause inoperative HVAC mode switch.
Answer D is correct because an open blower resistor will not affect mode switch operation.

Question #72
Answer A is wrong because some ATC microprocessors can be replaced independently from the control panel.
Answer B is wrong because many ATC microprocessors are integral to the control panel.
Answer C is correct because both technicians are right.
Answer D is wrong because one technician is right.

Question #73
Answer A is wrong because it does have an odor.
Answer B is correct because R-134a has a faint ether-like odor.
Answer C is wrong because R-134a has a faint ether-like odor.
Answer D is wrong because R-134a has a faint ether-like odor.

Question #74
Answer A is wrong because the A/C system must be completely evacuated before the compressor lubricant level is checked.
Answer B is correct because the A/C compressor must be operated just prior to removal to ensure that the refrigeration lubricant is properly distributed through the system.
Answer C is wrong because the compressor must be removed to check the lubricant level.
Answer D is wrong because the old lubricant must be drained into a calibrated container to determine the amount of fresh lubricant to be installed.

Question #75
Answer A is wrong because a seal pick should never be used to install A/C hose O-rings.
Answer B is wrong because refrigeration oil is the only acceptable lubricant for A/C system O-rings and seals.
Answer C is wrong because both technicians are wrong.
Answer D is correct because neither technician is right.

Question #76
Answer A is correct because cooling and heating system hoses do not need to be replaced because they look old.
Answer B is wrong because cracked hoses must be replaced.
Answer C is wrong because bulging hoses must be replaced.
Answer D is wrong because spongy hoses must be replaced.

Question #77
Answer A is wrong because the engine control unit can control an electric condenser fan motor.
Answer B is wrong because the body control unit can control an electric condenser fan motor.
Answer C is correct because a manual switch does not control an electric condenser fan.
Answer D is wrong because an electric condenser fan motor can be controlled by an electronic relay.

Question #78
Answer A is wrong because a kinked cable housing will cause the cable to bind.
Answer B is wrong because corrosion in the cable housing will cause the cable to bind.
Answer C is wrong because a deformed or overtightened cable clamp will cause the cable to bind.
Answer D is correct because the mode doors are not controlled by the temperature control cable.

Question #79
Answer A is wrong because the refrigerant does not need to be evacuated from the system before the valve is replaced.
Answer B is correct because the heater hoses connected to the coolant control valve may be clamped during the replacement procedure to maintain coolant in the system.
Answer C is wrong because the coolant control valve is located in front of the firewall.
Answer D is wrong because the coolant control valve is an individually replaceable component.

Question #80
Answer A is correct because a saline solution will cause corrosion.
Answer B is wrong because a soft whisk broom can be used to remove debris from the condenser fins
Answer C is wrong because compressed air can be used to remove debris from the condenser fins.
Answer D is wrong because a soap and water solution can be used to remove debris from the condenser fins.

Question #81
Answer A is correct because the thermal bulb must be in contact with the evaporator inlet or core.
Answer B is wrong because this area is the wrong location.
Answer C is wrong because this area is the wrong location.
Answer D is wrong because this area is the wrong location.

Question #82
Answer A is wrong because oil is not added to the heater core prior to installation.
Answer B is wrong because oil is not added to the heater core prior to installation.
Answer C is wrong because both technicians are wrong.
Answer D is correct because neither technician is right.

Question #83
Answer A is wrong because an open circuit is indicated by an FMI of 5.
Answer B is wrong because a short circuit to ground is indicated by an FMI of 4.
Answer C is correct because this failure code indicates a module failure.
Answer D is wrong because a loose connector would probably be indicated by multiple FMIs.

Question #84
Answer A is wrong because there is no need to remove control cables from the vehicle before replacing an electrical control panel.
Answer B is correct because the technician should disconnect the batteries before replacing an electric control panel.
Answer C is wrong because HVAC electric control panels can be replaced without disassembling the dash panels.
Answer D is wrong because nothing should be applied to the switch contacts.

Question #85
Answer A is wrong because a short circuit in the blower circuit could cause a blown fuse.
Answer B is wrong because a short circuit in an actuator motor could cause a blown fuse.
Answer C is correct because a shorted ECT sensor will cause a code to set, but will not blow a fuse.
Answer D is wrong because a damaged connector could cause a short circuit and blow a fuse.

Question #86
Answer A is wrong because a cobalt blue moisture sensor indicates that the refrigerant is not carrying any moisture.
Answer B is wrong because a cobalt blue moisture sensor indicates that the refrigerant is not carrying any moisture.
Answer C is wrong because both technicians are wrong.
Answer D is correct because neither technician is right.

Question #87
Answer A is wrong because the screws do not contact the diaphragm.
Answer B is correct because overtightening the mounting screws can result in stripped screw holes.
Answer C is wrong because this will have no effect on the linkage.
Answer D is wrong because a vacuum leak will not result of overtorqued screws.

Question #88
Answer A is wrong because the relief valve cannot be calibrated.
Answer B is wrong because the relief valve does not need to be replaced if it vents refrigerant to the atmosphere and then resets itself.
Answer C is correct because the system will reset itself when A/C system pressure returns to a safe level.
Answer D is wrong because all mobile A/C systems use a high-pressure relief valve.

Question #89
Answer A is wrong because a defective coolant control valve could cause this problem.
Answer B is correct because a defective engine coolant temperature sensor is least likely cause.
Answer C is wrong because a defective air control solenoid could cause this problem.
Answer D is wrong because a defective blend air door air cylinder could cause this problem.

Question #90
Answer A is wrong because the vapor line carries vaporized refrigerant back to the compressor.
Answer B is wrong because the condenser carries high pressure liquid.
Answer C is correct because the sudden increase in inside diameter of the A/C line at the orifice causes a radical pressure drop, allowing most of the refrigerant to vaporize instantly at that point. Any refrigerant that remains in the liquid state after it passes through the orifice, is quickly vaporized in the evaporator.
Answer D is wrong because the capillary tube is a temperature sensor and does not contain refrigerant.

Question #91
Answer A is a good choice because a suction throttling valve not regulating properly can cause reduced air flow from the instrument panel outlets, but A is wrong because both technicians are right.
Answer B is a good choice because a suction throttling valve not regulating properly could cause the evaporator to ice up, but is wrong because both technicians are right.
Answer C is correct because both technicians are right.
Answer D is wrong because both technicians are right.

Question #92
Answer A is correct because the standard coolant heated heater core type of heater is a forced air convection system.
Answer B is wrong because an immersion heater is sometimes used to preheat engine coolant.
Answer C is wrong because fuel-fired heaters are still uncommon in the United States.
Answer D is wrong because electric heaters are not practical for mobile HVAC systems.

Question #93
Answer A is wrong because the answer specifies the wrong data.
Answer B is correct because DOT 4BA-300 is the level of approval necessary for refrigerant recovery containers.
Answer C is wrong because the answer specifies the wrong data.
Answer D is wrong because the answer specifies the wrong data.

Question #94
Answer A is correct because when the compressor clutch is not engaged, the pressure in the A/C system equalizes.
Answer B is wrong because a restriction in the expansion valve will cause low, but not identical, system pressures.
Answer C is wrong because only technician A is right.
Answer D is wrong because one of the technicians is right.

Question #95
Answer A is wrong because compression fittings are not used in mobile A/C systems.
Answer B is correct because R-134a systems use SAE quick-connect couplings.
Answer C is wrong because different fittings are used to prevent mixing refrigerants.
Answer D is wrong because the size is not 10 mm.

Question #96
Answer A is wrong because cylinder pressure is not an accurate measure of contents level.
Answer B is correct because the total weight of the cylinder must not exceed the weight of the cylinder when it is empty plus the maximum rated net weight.
Answer C is wrong because refrigerant cylinders are not equipped with safety relief valves.
Answer D is wrong because shaking the cylinder is not an accurate measure of contents level.

Question #97
Answer A is wrong because 20 minutes is not enough time to evacuate.
Answer B is wrong because 10 minutes is not enough time to evacuate.
Answer C is wrong because 15 minutes is not enough time to evacuate.
Answer D is correct because to ensure that the entire system is under deep enough vacuum to remove all moisture, the pump should be run for at least 30 minutes.

Question #98
Answer A is wrong because methane is a flammable gas produced by rotting vegetation.
Answer B is correct because ozone in the upper atmosphere helps shield the earth from UV radiation.
Answer C is wrong because nitrogen makes up most of the air we breathe and is important as an atmospheric fire suppressant.
Answer D is wrong because argon is an inert gas used as flux in some welding processes.

Question #99
Answer A is wrong because when servicing a system with the type of service valve shown in the figure, the compressor can be isolated.
Answer B is wrong because the valve shown in the figure only permits reading of the suction and discharge pressures when it is in the mid-position or service position.
Answer C is wrong because both technicians are wrong.
Answer D is correct because both technicians are incorrect for the above reasons.

Question #100
Answer A is wrong because R-12 is not flammable.
Answer B is wrong because the gas that is formed is toxic, attacking the nervous system.
Answer C is wrong because R-12 does not form chlorine gas in the presence of a flame.
Answer D is correct because heated R-12 will form phosgene gas.

Question #101
Answer A is correct because refrigerant returns to the compressor as a low pressure gas.
Answer B is wrong because refrigerant in an operating A/C system is never a low pressure liquid.
Answer C is wrong because refrigerant leaves the compressor as a high pressure gas.
Answer D is wrong because refrigerant in the liquid line is a high pressure liquid.

Question #102
Answer A is wrong because phosgene gas forms when R-12 comes in contact with a flame.
Answer B is correct because when the system is purged too quickly, the refrigerant oil will atomize and travel from the system with the refrigerant.
Answer C is wrong because only one of the technicians is right.
Answer D is wrong because one of the technicians is right.

Question #103
Answer A is correct because in the MAX A/C mode the outside air door is closed.
Answer B is wrong because the defroster door is closed in the MAX A/C mode.
Answer C is wrong because the compressor clutch will cycle normally in the MAX A/C mode.
Answer D is wrong because the blower functions normally in the MAX A/C mode.

Question #104
Answer A is correct because an internal compressor leak could cause these symptoms.
Answer B is wrong because an overcharge of refrigerant oil will not cause these symptoms but will reduce the cooling capabilities of the system.
Answer C is wrong because only technician A is right.
Answer D is wrong because one of the technicians is right.

Question #105
Answer A is wrong because A/C system pressures vary with altitude.
Answer B is wrong because A/C system pressures vary with ambient temperature.
Answer C is wrong because A/C system pressures vary with barometric pressure.
Answer D is correct because A/C system pressures do not vary with cab temperature.

Question #106
Answer A is wrong because the thermostatic switch senses temperature at the evaporator inlet, and disengages the compressor clutch when evaporator icing is imminent.
Answer B is wrong because the EPR valve regulates the flow of refrigerant into the evaporator, preventing icing.
Answer C is wrong because the STV regulates the flow of refrigerant into the evaporator, preventing icing.
Answer D is correct because the low pressure cut-out switch prevents compressor damage due to a loss of refrigerant.

Question #107
Answer A is wrong because the TXV is to the right of the correct component.
Answer B is wrong because the figure does not show an EE-VIR unit.
Answer C is wrong because the figure does not show an EPR valve.
Answer D is correct because the component shown is a suction throttling valve (STV).

Question #108
Answer A is wrong because the POA valve is located near the evaporator.
Answer B is wrong because a filter is generally used on the suction side of the compressor.
Answer C is wrong because the ETR is located near the evaporator.
Answer D is correct because the indicated component is a muffler used to reduce compressor noise.

Question #109
Answer A is wrong because the binary switch also provides high pressure protection.
Answer B is wrong because the binary switch also provides high pressure protection.
Answer C is correct because the binary switch disables the A/C compressor when the system pressure is too high or too low.
Answer D is wrong because it does provide protection for the compressor in a low or high pressure situation.

Question #110
Answer A is wrong because the orifice tube is located in the evaporator core inlet.
Answer B is correct because the orifice tube provides for the rapid expansion, and thus evaporation, of the high pressure liquid refrigerant in the liquid line.
Answer C is wrong because the orifice tube does not affect the refrigerant flow through the condenser.
Answer D is wrong because the expansion valve does not affect air flow through the evaporator.

Question #111
Answer A is wrong because the cycling switch does not sense temperature.
Answer B is correct because the cycling switch is mounted in the accumulator where it senses pressure.
Answer C is wrong because the cycling switch senses accumulator pressure, not temperature.
Answer D is wrong because the cycling switch does not sense engine ambient temperature.

Question #112
Answer A is wrong because a refrigerant overcharge will cause high system pressures.
Answer B is wrong because an overheated engine will cause elevated high-side pressure due to high evaporator temperature.
Answer C is wrong because a restricted air flow through the condenser will cause elevated high-side pressure due to high evaporator temperature.
Answer D is correct because a blockage of the orifice tube screen will cause low, high-side pressure.

Question #113
Answer A is wrong because the sensor tip should be as close as possible to the fitting.
Answer B is correct because refrigerant is heavier than air, so it is most easily detected just below a leaking fitting.
Answer C is wrong because you place the sensor probe just below the fitting.
Answer D is wrong because you place the sensor probe just below the fitting.

Question #114
Answer A is wrong because a defective clutch will not cycle too fast.
Answer B is wrong because a defective switch will not cause this symptom.
Answer C is wrong because an overcharged system is more likely to cause the clutch to remain engaged.
Answer D is correct because low refrigerant charge will cause the clutch to cycle more frequently than normal.

Question #115
Answer A is wrong because the reed valves allow the compressor to draw refrigerant in from the system low side, compress it, and exhaust it to the system high side.
Answer B is wrong because the valves direct the flow of refrigerant.
Answer C is wrong because the valves direct the flow of refrigerant.
Answer D is correct because the valves direct the flow of refrigerant.

Question #116
Answer A is correct because the appropriate service manual should always be consulted for the manufacturer's specific instructions.
Answer B is wrong because the current refrigerant type can be identified by comparing the service valves.
Answer C is wrong because the warranty status of the vehicle is irrelevant to making the repair.
Answer D is wrong because previously replaced parts do not affect the retrofit procedure.

Question #117
Answer A is correct because the correct mix of 85% of the output air is directed to the windshield in the DEFROST mode. A 50/50 mix will result in a very slow windshield defrost.
Answer B is wrong because 85% of the output air directed to the windshield in the DEFROST mode is the appropriate mix.
Answer C is wrong because the mix is close enough to defrost the windshield.
Answer D is wrong because the mix is close enough to defrost the windshield.

Question #118
Answer A is wrong because one uses this method for finding leaks in the chassis air system and soapy solutions will not show refrigerant leaks.
Answer B is correct because an electronic leak detector is the most accurate method of leak detection.
Answer C is wrong because a flame-type leak detector provides only subjective results and in some locations is illegal.
Answer D is wrong because to use a black light detector, the technician must introduce dye into the A/C system and hope that any leaks are in an area that is viewable.

Question #119
Answer A is correct because if the expansion valve is stuck closed, the low side of the system will be pulled down into a vacuum and the compressor will not be able to sufficiently pressurize the high side.
Answer B is wrong because without flow, the compressor cannot generate high pressure.
Answer C is wrong because with the low side being depressed the low-side pressure will be nearing a vacuum.
Answer D is wrong because without flow, the compressor cannot generate high pressure.

Question #120
Answer A is correct because an open resistor is the most common cause of a blower motor inoperative in one or more speeds.
Answer B is wrong because an intermittent short will affect all blower speeds.
Answer C is wrong because a loose contact in the switch is possible, but not likely.
Answer D is wrong because a loose connector will affect all blower speeds.

Question #121
Answer A is wrong because a faint hissing noise after shutting down the engine is caused by the equalization of refrigerant pressure in the A/C system.
Answer B is wrong because this is a normal condition and a defective EPR valve causes evaporator freezing and poor cooling.
Answer C is wrong because neither technician is right.
Answer D is correct because this is a normal condition and both technicians are wrong.

Question #122
Answer A is a good choice but wrong, because both technicians are right.
Answer B is also a good choice but wrong, because both technicians are right.
Answer C is correct because fuel-fired heaters are rather new to the United States and fuel-fired heaters burn less fuel than running the engine at idle.
Answer D is wrong because both technicians are right.

Question #123
Answer A is wrong because in properly maintained cooling systems, clogged heater cores are rare.
Answer B is wrong because control units are relatively reliable.
Answer C is wrong because heater control valves do fail, but this is not the most common problem in HVAC systems.
Answer D is correct because coolant leaks are the most common problem in HVAC systems.

Question #124
Answer A is wrong because the blend air type HVAC system modulates temperature control by mixing the flow of air into the cab from the heater core and the A/C evaporator.
Answer B is wrong because ATC systems control all aspects of the HVAC system with a single input from the driver.
Answer C is correct because chilling and heating water and then recirculating it are only used in stationary HVAC systems.
Answer D is wrong because SATC systems require the driver to set the temperature and control the blower speed.

Question #125
Answer A is wrong because original refrigerant containers should not be used to store recycled refrigerant.
Answer B is wrong because if the valve is simply opened, any remaining refrigerant will be vented to the atmosphere.
Answer C is wrong because there is no reason to introduce oil into the cylinder.
Answer D is correct because after any remaining refrigerant is recovered, the cylinder should be evacuated, marked, and recycled for scrap metal.

Question #126
Answer A is wrong because there are many tools required to properly diagnose HVAC system failures.
Answer B is correct because a small thermometer can be used to monitor the performance of an HVAC system.
Answer C is wrong because only one of the technicians is right.
Answer D is wrong because one of the technicians is right.

Question #127
Answer A is wrong because 5–10 psi is an extremely low, low-side pressure indicative of a clogged orifice tube or low refrigerant charge.
Answer B is correct because 25–45 is the normal low-side pressure.
Answer C is wrong because 60–80 psi is a very high, low-side pressure.
Answer D is wrong because 180–205 psi is a typical high-side pressure.

Question #128
Answer A is wrong because excessive pressure in the system would have to be high enough to rupture a hose, and that is unlikely.
Answer B is correct because refrigerant leaking from a hose connection will usually contain some refrigeration oil, which quickly collects dirt.
Answer C is wrong because a shaft seal will only cause an oil residue at the front of the compressor.
Answer D is wrong because too much oil in the system reduces system efficiency and causes low cooling because the system cannot depress the oil.

Question #129
Answer A is correct because if the expansion valve is stuck open, the low-side pressure will be high and the compressor will run continuously.
Answer B is wrong because a system having a high, low-side reading accompanied by a continuously running compressor, indicates that the expansion valve is NOT operating properly.
Answer C is wrong because only one technician is right.
Answer D is wrong because one of the technicians is right.

Question #130
Answer A is wrong because a worn out compressor clutch coil will not cause the clutch to slip.
Answer B is wrong because a defective relay will prevent the clutch from engaging.
Answer C is correct because if the air gap is too large, the clutch may slip briefly upon engagement.
Answer D is wrong because a worn clutch bearing may cause a loud clutch engagement but not a slipping clutch.

Question #131
Answer A is wrong because in a semi-automatic temperature control system, mode selection is a manual operation.
Answer B is wrong because the blend door actuator is responsible for temperature control only.
Answer C is wrong because the blower system does not affect mode selection.
Answer D is correct because an improperly adjusted cable could affect the amount of air that is directed toward the windshield.

Question #132
Answer A is correct because the orifice tube screen is installed to prevent particulate from circulating through the system in the event that the desiccant bag in the receiver/drier breaks down.
Answer B is wrong because atomization is not important to the evaporation of refrigerant, only fuel.
Answer C is wrong because only technician A is right.
Answer D is wrong because one of the technicians is right.

Question #133
Answer A is correct because the compressor discharge valve opens after the pressure compresses the vaporous refrigerant, allowing the refrigerant to move to the condenser.
Answer B is wrong because if the discharge valve opened before the vaporous refrigerant compressed, it would not properly raise the refrigerant pressure to allow a change from gas to a liquid. In addition, it does not go to the evaporator.
Answer C is wrong because the reed valves just open and close, they do not regulate a variable pressure.
Answer D is wrong because reed valves cannot sense A/C system temperature, so regulation can not take place.

Question #134
Answer A is a good choice because you must remove the evaporator to check lubricant level, but wrong because both technicians are right.
Answer B is a good choice because first you run the A/C compressor briefly, to ensure that the refrigeration oil distributes throughout the system, but wrong because both technicians are right.
Answer C is correct because both technicians are right.
Answer D is wrong because neither technician is wrong.

Question #135
Answer A is correct because restricted air flow through the condenser will cause elevated high-side pressure.
Answer B is wrong because a thermostat stuck open will not cause elevated high-side pressure.
Answer C is wrong because the thermal bulb will not leak.
Answer D is wrong because the bypass valve is a component in thermactor air cleaner.

Question #136
Answer A is wrong because it is important to remove moisture from the A/C system before charging the system, because moisture will combine with the refrigerant and develop into an acid, and the compressor will suffer excessive wear.
Answer B is correct because moisture that enters the A/C system will be harmful to the system and cause poor performance because of internal erosion and the inability of the system to pull down the pressure.
Answer C is wrong because only one of the technicians is right.
Answer D is wrong because one of the technicians is right.

Question #137

Answer A is correct because some manufacturers do recommend this practice of installing an in-line filter.

Answer B is wrong because the filter that contains an orifice replaces the original orifice tube. If you do not remove the original orifice, an restriction will result with poor performance.

Answer C is wrong because only one of the technicians is right.

Answer D is wrong because one of the technicians is right.

Question #138

Answer A is wrong because if you complete the charging process with the engine running, liquid refrigerant may enter the compressor with resulting damage.

Answer B is correct because you cannot compress liquid refrigerant because it will result in damage.

Answer C is wrong because only technician B is right.

Answer D is wrong because one of the technicians is right.

Question #139

Answer A is wrong because one completes the charging process when the correct weight of refrigerant has entered the system.

Answer B is wrong because if the low side does not move from a vacuum to a pressure, there is a restriction.

Answer C is wrong because the truck engine does not need to be running during recharging.

Answer D is correct because OEM's recommend either a high-side (liquid) or a low-side (vapor) charging process.

Question #140

Answer A is wrong because only R-12 A/C systems use mineral oil.

Answer B is wrong because PAG oil is a synthetic lubricant used in R-134a A/C systems.

Answer C is wrong because both technicians are wrong.

Answer D is correct because neither technician is right.

Question #141

Answer A is a good choice because the tool shown in the figure is used as shaft seal protector, but is wrong because both technicians are right.

Answer B is also a good choice because the seal seat O-ring must be installed before the shaft seal, but is wrong because both technicians are right.

Answer C is correct because both technicians are right.

Answer D is wrong because both technicians are right.

Question #142

Answer A is wrong because a plugged evaporator case may cause windshield fogging, but this problem would not result in an oily film on the windshield.

Answer B is correct because a refrigerant leak in the evaporator case may allow some refrigerant and oil to leak and cause a thin oily film on the windshield.

Answer C is wrong because only one technician is right.

Answer D is wrong because one technician is right.

Question #143

Answer A is wrong because the service valve is front seated and this blocks the gauge port so no pressure would register on a manifold gauge set. One uses the service valve mid-position for service.

Answer B is wrong because the system could not operate normally because the passage to the compressor is blocked. Some system pressure may appear at the gauge port. You back seat the service valve for normal operation.

Answer C is correct because front seating a service valve isolates the compressor from the system for service.

Answer D is wrong because pressure form the compressor is blocked. One uses the service valve mid-position for service.

Question #144
Answer A is a good choice because a sticky film is an indication of and engine coolant leak, but wrong because both technicians are right.
Answer B is a good choice because the heater core has coolant running through it and it is located inside the truck and could put a sticky film on the inside of the windshield, but wrong because both technicians are right.
Answer C is correct because both technicians are right.
Answer D is wrong because both technicians are right.

Question #145
Answer A is wrong because an overheating engine will result in the exact opposite condition; i.e., a lean condition.
Answer B is wrong because a defective radiator cap will cause engine overheating.
Answer C is correct because with the engine thermostat stuck open, the engine will not reach operating temperature. This will result in the engine coolant sensor sending a cold engine message to the computer resulting in a rich air–fuel mix.
Answer D is wrong because a stuck open coolant valve only affects truck interior heating.

Question #146
Answer A is wrong because when the cooling system pressure is increased, the boiling point increases.
Answer B is correct because if one adds more antifreeze to the coolant, the boiling point increases.
Answer C is wrong because a good quality ethylene glycol antifreeze contains antirust inhibitors.
Answer D is wrong because coolant solutions must be recovered, recycled, and handled as hazardous waste.

Question #147
Answer A is wrong because SCA stands for supplemental coolant additive which is a corrosion inhibitor additive. Adding more antifreeze does not change the SCA reading.
Answer B is wrong because continuing to run the truck until the next PMI will not change the SCA reading.
Answer C is correct because one needs to drain the entire coolant system and add the proper SCA mixture to achieve the correct percentage of SCA.
Answer D is wrong because this will not change SCA readings.

Question #148
Answer A is wrong because the figure does not show the air mix door adjustment .
Answer B is correct because the figure shows the manual coolant valve adjustment.
Answer C is wrong because the figure does not show the ventilation door control rod adjustment.
Answer D is wrong because the figure does not show the defroster door control rod adjustment.

Question #149
Answer A is a good choice because fast idle solenoids typically have an adjustment. If this adjustment sets the computer applied idle speed too low or adjustment steps were missed, the engine may stall with A/C compressor engaged, but A is wrong because both technicians are right.
Answer B is also a good choice because the fuel management computer typically operates this device, but B is wrong because both technicians are right.
Answer C is correct because both technicians are right.
Answer D is wrong because one technician is right.

Question #150
Answer A is an accurate statement because some actuator motors are calibrated automatically in the self-diagnostic mode. Therefore, it is wrong.
Answer B is correct because it is the EXCEPTION statement and A/C diagnostic trouble codes (DTC) represent a fault in a specific system, not a component.
Answer C is an accurate statement because the actuator control rods must be calibrated manually on some systems. Therefore, it is also wrong.
Answer D is an accurate statement because the actuator motor control rods should only require adjustment after motor replacement or adjustment. However, because it is a true statement, it is wrong.

Question #151
Answer A is wrong because the question asks for the statement that is not true and you do remove the negative battery cable before control panel service.
Answer B is correct because this is the incorrect statement. You do not discharge the refrigerant before removing the control panel.
Answer C is wrong because the question asks for the statement that is not true. If the truck contains a supplemental restraint system, wait the specified period after you remove the negative battery cable.
Answer D is wrong because the question asks for the statement that is not true and self-diagnostic tests may indicate a defective control panel in an ATC system.

Question #152
Answer A is wrong because a leaking dash vacuum switch will hiss and cause some control problems but will not cause total loss of vacuum control to the mode doors.
Answer B is wrong because a defective A/C compressor would cause total loss of any cold air.
Answer C is correct because the loss of vacuum supply to the control panel results in a fail-safe mode of all air to the lower heater outlets.
Answer D is wrong because a heater control valve failure causes either no cold air or no hot air.

Question #153
Answer A is wrong because you test control panel vacuum systems by applying vacuum with a hand pump to the input end of the system, not output.
Answer B is correct because you connect the vacuum pump to each vacuum actuator and supply 15 to 20 in. Hg. to the actuator and the gauge should stay at a steady vacuum for 1 minute.
Answer C is wrong because only one technician is right.
Answer D is wrong because one technician is right.

Question #154
Answer A is correct because the check valve is a one-way valve that allows the reservoir to hold constant vacuum regardless of fluctuations in the vacuum source.
Answer B is wrong because a bad vacuum pump would cause this condition constantly, not just on shut down and uphill.
Answer C is wrong because bad fuel injectors may affect engine operation under load, but not during shut down.
Answer D is wrong because a leaking actuator diaphragm would cause this condition all of the time.

Question #155
Answer A is correct because when recirculation door is in position A, outside air is drawn into the HVAC case.
Answer B is wrong because in position A in vehicle air is blocked.
Answer C is wrong because only one technician is right.
Answer D is wrong because one technician is right.

Question #156
Answer A is a good choice because a defective in car sensor would cause this condition. However, it is wrong because both technicians are right.
Answer B is also a good choice because a sticking air blend door can also cause this condition. However, it is wrong because both technicians are right.
Answer C is correct because both technicians are right.
Answer D is wrong because one technician is right.

Question #157
Answer A is wrong because the question asks for a defect that is NOT the cause of the problem and a seized water control valve in the heater hose may cause the water control to move with 16 inches of vacuum supplied.
Answer B is wrong because the question asks for a defect that is NOT the cause of the problem and a plugged vacuum hose between the solenoid and valve may cause the water control to move with 16 inches of vacuum supplied.
Answer C is wrong because the question asks for a defect that is NOT the cause of the problem and a plugged vacuum hose between the solenoid and valve may cause the water control to move with 16 inches of vacuum supplied.
Answer D is correct because a seized plunger in the water valve control solenoid will cause the plunger not to move.

Question #158
Answer A is wrong because in a strategy-based diagnostic process of elimination, you must check for visual signs before replacing any parts.
Answer B is correct because the first process is a visual one to check the components.
Answer C is wrong because one technician is right.
Answer D is wrong because one technician is right.

Question #159
Answer A is correct because it is the most likely due to the fact that the resistance check showed the circuit to be good, nulling answers C and D.
Answer B is wrong because it is much less likely to have failed than answer A.
Answer C is also wrong because an ohmmeter connected to terminals 9 and 18 in the control panel connector indicates the circuit is good.
Answer D is wrong because the ohmmeter that is connected to terminals 9 and 18 in the control panel connector indicates the circuit is good.

Question #160
Answer A is wrong because replacing the ATC control computer should only take place after following specific diagnostic steps.
Answer B is correct because you should follow and perform the diagnostic steps in the truck manufacturer's service manual.
Answer C is wrong because only one technician is right.
Answer D is wrong because one of the technicians is right.

Question #161
Answer A is correct because it is the lowest value in the choices and represents the maximum voltage drop allowed across a ground at 1/10 of volt.
Answer B is wrong because the drop is too large with resultant high resistance.
Answer C is wrong because the drop is too large with resultant high resistance.
Answer D is wrong because the drop is too large with resultant high resistance.

Question #162
Answer A is a true statement because the equipment label must indicate UL approval; therefore, it is wrong.
Answer B is a true statement because the equipment label must indicate SAE J1991 approval; therefore, it is wrong.
Answer C is correct. The statement is false because you must use the specified type of refrigerant storage container in this equipment.
Answer D is a true statement because R-12 and R-134a refrigerants or refrigerant oils must not be mixed in the recovery/recycling process; therefore, it is wrong.

Question #163
Answer A is wrong because moisture is detrimental to an A/C system because it combines with the refrigerant and becomes corrosive.
Answer B is correct because moisture that enters the A/C system will cause internal corrosion. Additionally, moisture can accumulate on the expansion valve or orifice tube and freeze, blocking the flow of refrigerant and preventing proper performance.
Answer C is wrong because only technician B is right.
Answer D is wrong because one of the technicians is right.

Glossary

ABS An abbreviation for Anti-lock Brake System.

Absolute Pressure The aero point from which pressure is measured.

Ackerman Principle The geometric principle used to provide toe-out on turns. The ends of the steering arms are angled so that the inside wheel turns more than the outside wheel when a vehicle is making a turn.

Actuator A device that delivers motion in response to an electrical signal.

Adapter The welds under a spring seat to increase the mounting height or fit a seal to the axle.

Adapter Ring A part that is bolted between the clutch cover and the flywheel on some two-plate clutches when the clutch is installed on a flat flywheel.

A/D Converter An abbreviation for Analog-to-Digital Converter.

Additive An additive intended to improve a certain characteristic of the material.

Adjustable Torque Arm A member used to retain axle alignment and, in some cases, control axle torque. Normally one adjustable and one rigid torque arm are used per axle so the axle can be aligned. This rod has means by which it can be extended or retracted for adjustment purposes.

Adjusting Ring A device that is held in the shift signal valve bore by a press fit pin through the valve body housing. When the ring is pushed in by the adjusting tool, the slots on the ring that engage the pin are released.

After-Cooler A device that removes water and oil from the air by a cooling process. The air leaving an after-cooler is saturated with water vapor, which condenses when a drop in temperature occurs.

Air Bag An air-filled device that functions as the spring on axles that utilize air pressure in the suspension system.

Air Brakes A braking system that uses air pressure to actuate the brakes by means of diaphragms, wedges, or cams.

Air Brake System A system utilizing compressed air to activate the brakes.

Air Compressor (1) An engine-driven mechanism for supplying high pressure air to the truck brake system. There are basically two types of compressors: those designed to work on in-line engines and those that work on V-type engines. The in-line type is mounted forward and is gear driven, while the V-type is mounted toward the firewall and is camshaft driven. With both types the coolant and lubricant are supplied by the truck engine. (2) A pump-like device in the air conditioning system that compresses refrigerant vapor to achieve a change in state for the refrigeration process.

Air Conditioning The control of air movement, humidity, and temperature by mechanical means.

Air Dryer A unit that removes moisture.

Air Filter/Regulator Assembly A device that minimizes the possibility of moisture-laden air or impurities entering a system.

Air Hose An air line, such as one between the tractor and trailer, that supplies air for the trailer brakes.

Air-Over-Hydraulic Brakes A brake system utilizing a hydraulic system assisted by an air pressure system.

Air-Over-Hydraulic Intensifier A device that changes the pneumatic air pressure from the treadle brake valve into hydraulic pressure which controls the wheel cylinders.

Air Shifting The process that uses air pressure to engage different range combinations in the transmission's auxiliary section without a mechanical linkage to the driver.

Air Slide Release A release mechanism for a sliding fifth wheel, which is operated from the cab of a tractor by actuating an air control valve. When actuated, the valve energizes an air cylinder, which releases the slide lock and permits positioning of the fifth wheel.

Air Spring An airfilled device that functions as the spring on axles that utilize air pressure in the suspension system.

Air Spring Suspension A single or multi-axle suspension relying on air bags for springs and weight distribution of axles.

Air Timing The time required for the air to be transmitted to or released from each brake, starting the instant the driver moves the brake pedal.

Altitude Compensation System An altitude barometric switch and solenoid used to provide better driveability at more than 4,000 feet (1220 meters) above sea level.

Ambient Temperature Temperature of the surrounding or prevailing air. Normally, it is considered to be the temperature in the service area where testing is taking place.

Amboid Gear A gear that is similar to the hypoid type with one exception: the axis of the drive pinion gear is located above the centerline axis of the ring gear.

Amp An abbreviation for ampere.

Ampere The unit for measuring electrical current.

Analog Signal A voltage signal that varies within a given range (from high to low, including all points in between).

Analog-to-Digital Converter (A/D converter) A device that converts analog voltage signals to a digital format; this is located in a section of the processor called the input signal conditioner.

Analog Volt/Ohmmeter (AVOM) A test meter used for checking voltage and resistance. Analog meters should not be used on solid state circuits.

Annulus The largest part of a simple gear set.

Anticorrosion Agent A chemical used to protect metal surfaces from corrosion.

Antifreeze A compound, such as alcohol or glycerin, that is added to water to lower its freezing point.

Anti-lock Brake System (ABS) A computer controlled brake system having a series of sensing devices at each wheel that control braking action to prevent wheel lockup.

Anti-lock Relay Valve (ARV) In an anti-lock brake system, the device that usually replaces the standard relay valve used to control the rear axle service brakes and performs the standard relay function during tractor/trailer operation.

Antirattle Springs Springs that reduce wear between the intermediate plate and the drive pin, and helps to improve clutch release.

Antirust Agent An additive used with lubricating oils to prevent rusting of metal parts when the engine is not in use.

Application Valve A foot-operated brake valve that controls air pressure to the service chambers.

Applied Moment A term meaning a given load has been placed on a frame at a particular point.

Area The total cross section of a frame rail including all applicable elements usually given in square inches.

Armature The rotating component of a (1) starter or other motor. (2) generator. (3) compressor clutch.

Articulating Upper Coupler A bolster plate kingpin arrangement that is not rigidly attached to the trailer, but provides articulation and/or oscillation, (such as a frameless dump) about an axis parallel to the rear axle of the trailer.

Articulation Vertical movement of the front driving or rear axle relative to the frame of the vehicle to which they are attached.

ASE An abbreviation for Automotive Service Excellence, a trademark of National Institute for Automotive Service Excellence.

Aspect Ratio A tire term calculated by dividing the tire's section height by its section width.

ATEC System A system that includes an electronic control system, torque converter, lockup clutch, and planetary gear train.

Atmospheric Pressure The weight of the air at sea level; 14.696 pounds per square inch (psi) or 101.33 kilopascals (kPa).

Automatic Slack Adjuster The device that automatically adjusts the clearance between the brake linings and the brake drum or rotor. The slack adjuster controls the clearance by sensing the length of the stroke of the push rod for the air brake chamber.

Autoshift Finger The device that engages the shift blocks on the yoke bars that corresponds to the tab on the end of the gearshift lever in manual systems.

Auxiliary Filter A device installed in the oil return line between the oil cooler and the transmission to prevent debris from being flushed into the transmission causing a failure. An auxiliary filter must be installed before the vehicle is placed back in service.

Auxiliary Section The section of a transmission where range shifting occurs, housing the auxiliary drive gear, auxiliary main shaft assembly, auxiliary countershaft, and the synchronizer assembly.

Axis of Rotation The center line around which a gear or part revolves.

Axle (1) A rod or bar on which wheels turn. (2) A shaft that transmits driving torque to the wheels.

Axle Range Interlock A feature designed to prevent axle shifting when the interaxle differential is locked out, or when lockout is engaged. The basic shift system operates the same as the standard shift system to shift the axle and engage or disengage the lockout.

Axle Seat A suspension component used to support and locate the spring on an axle.

Axle Shims Thin wedges that may be installed under the leaf springs of single axle vehicles to tilt the axle and correct the U-joint operating angles. Wedges are available in a range of sizes to change pinion angles.

Backing Plate A metal plate that serves as the foundation for the brake shoes and other drum brake hardware.

Battery Terminal A tapered post or threaded studs on top of the battery case, or infernally threaded provisions on the side of the battery for connecting the cables.

Beam Solid Mount Suspension A tandem suspension relying on a pivotal mounted beam, with axles attached at the ends for load equalization. The beam is mounted to a solid center pedestal.

Beam Suspension A tandem suspension relying on a pivotally mounted beam, with axles attached at ends for lead equalization. Beam is mounted to center spring.

Bellows A movable cover or seal that is pleated or folded like an accordion to allow for expansion and contraction.

Bending Moment A term implying that when a load is applied to the frame, it will be distributed across a given section of the frame material.

Bias A tire term where belts and plies are laid diagonally or crisscrossing each other.

Bimetallic Two dissimilar metals joined together that have different bending characteristics when subjected to different changes of temperature.

Blade Fuse A type of fuse having two flat male lugs sticking out for insertion in the female box connectors.

Bleed Air Tanks The process of draining condensation from air tanks to increase air capacity and brake efficiency.

Block Diagnosis Chart A troubleshooting chart that lists symptoms, possible causes, and probable remedies in columns.

Blower Fan A fan that pushes or blows air through a ventilation, heater, or air conditioning system.

Bobtail Proportioning Valve A valve that senses when the tractor is bobtailing and automatically reduces the amount of air pressure that can be applied to the tractor's drive axle(s). This reduces braking force on the drive axles, lessening the chance of a spin out on slippery pavement.

Bobtailing A tractor running without a trailer.

Bogie The axle spring, suspension arrangement on the rear of a tandem axle tractor.

Bolster Plate The flat load-bearing surface under the front of a semitrailer, including the kingpin, which rests firmly on the fifth wheel when coupled.

Bolster Plate Height The height from the ground to the bolster plate when the trailer is level and empty.

Boss A heavy cast section that is used for support, such as the outer race of a bearing.

Bottoming A condition that occurs when; (1) The teeth of one gear touch the lowest point between teeth of a mating gear. (2) The bed or frame of the vehicle strikes the axle, such as may be the case of overloading.

Bottom U-Bolt Plate A plate that is located on the bottom side of the spring or axle and is held in place when the U-bolts are tightened to the clamp spring and axle together.

Bracket An attachment used to secure parts to the body or frame.

Brake Control Valve A dual brake valve that releases air from the service reservoirs to the service lines and brake chambers. The valve includes a piston which pushes on diaphragms to open ports; these vent air to service lines in the primary and secondary systems.

Brake Disc A steel disc used in a braking system with a caliper and pads. When the brakes are applied, the pad on each side of the spinning disc is forced against the disc, thus imparting a braking force. This type of brake is very resistant to brake fade.

Brake Drum A cast metal bell-like cylinder attached to the wheel that is used to house the brake shoes and provide a friction surface for stopping a vehicle.

Brake Fade A condition that occurs when friction surfaces become hot enough to cause the coefficient of friction to drop to a point where the application of severe pedal pressure results in little actual braking.

Brake Lining A special friction material used to line brake shoes or brake pads. It withstands high temperatures and pressure. The molded material is either riveted or bonded to the brake shoe, with a suitable coefficient of friction for stopping a vehicle.

Brake Pad The friction lining and plate assembly that is forced against the rotor to cause braking action in a disc brake system.

Brake Shoe The curved metal part, faced with brake lining, which is forced against the brake drum to produce braking action.

Brake Shoe Rollers A hardware part that attaches to the web of the brake shoes by means of roller retainers. The rollers, in turn, ride on the end of an S-cam.

Brake System The vehicle system that slows or stops a vehicle. A combination of brakes and a control system.

Breakaway Valve A device that automatically seals off the tractor air supply from the trailer air supply when the tractor system pressure drops to 30 or 40 psi (207 or 276 kPa).

British Thermal Unit (Btu) A measure of heat quantity equal to the amount of heat required to raise 1 pound of water 1°F.

Broken Back Drive Shaft A term often used for non-parallel drive shaft.

Btu An abbreviation for British Thermal Unit.

Bump Steer Erratic steering caused from rolling over bumps, cornering, or heavy braking. Same as orbital steer and roll steer.

CAA An abbreviation for Clean Air Act.

Caliper A disc brake component that changes hydraulic pressure into mechanical force and uses that force to press the brake pads against the rotor and stop the vehicle. Calipers come in three basic types: fixed, floating, and sliding, and can have one or more pistons.

Camber The attitude of a wheel and tire assembly when viewed from the front of a car. If it leans outward, away from the car at the top, the wheel is said to have positive camber. If it leans inward, it is said to have negative camber.

Cam Brakes Brakes that are similar in operation and design to the wedge brake, with the exception that an S-type camshaft is used instead of a wedge and rubber assembly.

Cartridge Fuse A type of fuse having a strip of low melting point metal enclosed in a glass tube. If an excessive current flows through the circuit, the fuse element melts at the narrow portion, opening the circuit and preventing damage.

Caster The angle formed between the kingpin axis and a vertical axis as viewed from the side of the vehicle. Caster is considered positive when the top of the kingpin axis is behind the vertical axis.

Cavitation A condition that causes bubble formation.

Center of Gravity The point around which the weight of a truck is evenly distributed; the point of balance.

Ceramic Fuse A fuse found in some import vehicles that has a ceramic insulator with a conductive metal strip along one side.

CFC An abbreviation for chlorofluorocarbon.

Charging System A system consisting of the battery, alternator, voltage regulator, associated wiring, and the electrical loads of a vehicle. The purpose of the system is to recharge the battery whenever necessary and to provide the current required to power the electrical components.

Charge the Trailer To supply the trailer air tanks with air by means of a dash control valve, tractor protection valve, and a trailer relay emergency valve.

Charging Circuit The alternator (or generator) and associated circuit used to keep the battery charged and to furnish power to the vehicle's electrical systems when the engine is running.

Check Valve A valve that allows air to flow in one direction only. It is a federal requirement to have a check valve between the wet and dry air tanks.

Chlorofluorocarbon (CFC) A compound used in the production of refrigerant that is believed to cause damage to the ozone layer.

Circuit The complete path of an electrical current, including the generating device. When the path is unbroken, the circuit is closed and current flows. When the circuit continuity is broken, the circuit is open and current flow stops.

Clean Air Act (CAA) Federal regulations, passed in 1992, that have resulted in major changes in air-conditioning systems.

Climbing A gear problem caused by excessive wear in gears, bearings, and shafts whereby the gears move sufficiently apart to cause the apex (or point) of the teeth on one gear to climb over the apex of the teeth on another gear with which it is meshed.

Clutch A device for connecting and disconnecting the engine from the transmission or for a similar purpose in other units.

Clutch Brake A circular disc with a friction surface that is mounted on the transmission input spline between the release bearing and the transmission. Its purpose is to slow or stop the transmission input shaft from rotating in order to allow gears to be engaged without clashing or grinding.

Clutch Housing A component that surrounds and protects the clutch and connects the transmission case to the vehicle's engine.

Clutch Pack An assembly of normal clutch plates, friction discs, and one very thick plate known as the pressure plate. The pressure plate has tabs around the outside diameter to mate with the channel in the clutch drum.

COE An abbreviation for cab-over-engine.

Coefficient of Friction A measurement of the amount of friction developed between two objects in physical contact when one of the objects is drawn across the other.

Coil Springs Spring steel spirals that are mounted on control arms or axles to absorb road shock.

Combination A truck coupled to one or more trailers.

Compression Applying pressure to a spring or any springy substance, thus causing it to reduce its length in the direction of the compressing force.

Compressor (1) A mechanical device that increases pressure within a container by pumping air into it. (2) That component of an air-conditioning system that compresses low temperature/pressure refrigerant vapor.

Condensation The process by which gas (or vapor) changes to a liquid.

Condenser A component in an air-conditioning system used to cool a refrigerant below its boiling point causing it to change from a vapor to a liquid.

Conductor Any material that permits the electrical current to flow.

Constant Rate Springs Leaf-type spring assemblies that have a constant rate of deflection.

Control Arm The main link between the vehicle's frame and the wheels that acts as a hinge to allow wheel action up and down independent of the chassis.

Controlled Traction A type of differential that uses a friction plate assembly to transfer drive torque from the vehicle's slipping wheel to the one wheel that has good traction or surface bite.

Converter Dolly An axle, frame, drawbar, and fifth wheel arrangement that converts a semitrailer into a full trailer.

Coolant Liquid that circulates in an engine cooling system.

Coolant Heater A component used to aid engine starting and reduce the wear caused by cold starting.

Coolant Hydrometer A tester designed to measure coolant specific gravity and determine the amount of antifreeze in the coolant.

Cooling System Complete system for circulating coolant.

Coupling Point The point at which the turbine is turning at the same speed as the impeller.

Crankcase The housing within which the crankshaft and many other parts of the engine operate.

Cranking Circuit The starter and its associated circuit, including battery, relay (solenoid), ignition switch, neutral start switch (on vehicles with automatic transmission), and cables and wires.

Cross Groove Joint disc-shaped type of inner CV joint that uses balls and V-shaped grooves on the inner and outer races to accommodate the plunging motion of the half-shaft. The joint usually bolts to a transaxle stub flange; same as disc-type joint.

Cross-Tube A system that transfers the steering motion to the opposite, passenger side steering knuckle. It links the two steering knuckles together and forces them to act in unison.

C-Train A combination of two or more trailers in which the dolly is connected to the trailer by means of two pintle hook or coupler drawbar connections. The resulting connection has one pivot point.

Cycling (1) Repeated on-off action of the air conditioner compressor. (2) Heavy and repeated electrical cycling that can cause the positive plate material to break away from its grids and fall into the sediment chambers at the base of the battery case.

Dampen To slow or reduce oscillations or movement.

Dampened Discs Discs that have dampening springs incorporated into the disc hub. When engine torque is first transmitted to the disc, the plate rotates on the hub, compressing the springs. This action absorbs the shocks and torsional vibration caused by today's low rpm, high torque, engines.

Dash Control Valves A variety of handoperated valves located on the dash. They include parking brake valves, tractor protection valves, and differential lock.

Data Links Circuits through which computers communicate with other electronic devices such as control panels, modules, some sensors, or other computers in the form of digital signals.

Dead Axle Non-live or dead axles are often mounted in lifting suspensions. They hold the axle off the road when the vehicle is traveling empty, and put it on the road when a load is being carried. They are also used as air suspension third axles on heavy straight trucks and are used extensively in eastern states with high axle weight laws. An axle that does not rotate but merely forms a base on which to attach the wheels.

Deadline To take a vehicle out of service.

Deburring To remove sharp edges from a cut.

Dedicated Contract Carriage Trucking operations set up and run according to a specific shipper's needs. In addition to transportation, they often provide other services such as warehousing and logistics planning.

Deflection Bending or moving to a new position as the result of an external force.

Department of Transportation (DOT) A government agency that establishes vehicle standards.

Detergent Additive An additive that helps keep metal surfaces clean and prevents deposits. These additives suspend particles of carbon and oxidized oil in the oil.

DER An abbreviation for Department of Environmental Resources.

Diagnostic Flow Chart A chart that provides a systematic approach to the electrical system and component troubleshooting and repair. They are found in service manuals and are vehicle make and model specific.

Dial Caliper A measuring instrument capable of taking inside, outside, depth, and step measurements.

Differential A gear assembly that transmits power from the drive shaft to the wheels and allows two opposite wheels to turn at different speeds for cornering and traction.

Differential Carrier Assembly An assembly that controls the drive axle operation.

Differential Lock A toggle or push-pull type air switch that locks together the rear axles of a tractor so they pull as one for off-the-road operation.

Digital Binary Signal A signal that has only two values; on and off.

Digital Volt/Ohmmeter (DVOM) A type of test meter recommended by most manufacturers for use on solid state circuits.

Diode The simplest semiconductor device formed by joining P-type semiconductor material with N-type semiconductor material. A diode allows current to flow in one direction, but not in the opposite direction.

Direct Drive The gearing of a transmission so that in its highest gear, one revolution of the engine produces one revolution of the transmission's output shaft. The top gear or final drive ratio of a direct drive transmission would be 1:1.

Disc Brake A steel disc used in a braking system with a caliper and pads. When the brakes are applied, the pad on each side of the spinning disc is forced against the disc, thus imparting a braking force. This type of brake is very resistant to brake fade. A type of brake that generates stopping power by the application of pads against a rotating disc (rotor).

Dispatch Sheet A form used to keep track of dates when the work is to be completed. Some dispatch sheets follow the job through each step of the servicing process.

Dog Tracking Off-center tracking of the rear wheels as related to the front wheels.

DOT An abbreviation for Department of Transportation.

Downshift Control The selection of a lower range to match driving conditions encountered or expected to be encountered. Learning to take advantage of a downshift gives better control on slick or icy roads and on steep downgrades. Downshifting to lower ranges increases engine braking.

Double Reduction Axle An axle that uses two gear sets for greater overall gear reduction and peak torque development. This design is favored for severe service applications, such as dump trucks, cement mixers, and other heavy haulers.

Drag Link A connecting rod or link between the steering gear, Pitman arm, and the steering linkage.

Drawbar Capacity The maximum, horizontal pulling force that can be safely applied to a coupling device.

Driven Gear A gear that is driven or forced to turn by a drive gear, by a shaft, or by some other device.

Drive or Driving Gear A gear that drives another gear or causes another gear to turn.

Drive Line The propeller or drive shaft, universal joints, and so forth, that links the transmission output to the axle pinion gear shaft.

Drive Line Angle The alignment of the transmission output shaft, driveshaft, and rear axle pinion centerline.

Drive Shaft An assembly of one or two universal joints connected to a shaft or tube; used to transmit power from the transmission to the differential.

Drive Train An assembly that includes all power transmitting components from the rear of the engine to the wheels, including clutch/torque converter, transmission, drive line, and front and rear driving axles.

Driver Controlled Main Differential Lock A type of axle assembly has greater flexibility over the standard type of single reduction axle because it provides equal amounts of drive line torque to each driving wheel, regardless of changing road conditions. This design also provides the necessary differential action to the road wheels when the truck is turning a corner.

Driver's Manual A publication that contains information needed by the driver to understand, operate, and care for the vehicle and its components.

Drum Brake A type of brake system in which stopping friction is created by the shoes pressing against the inside of the rotating drum.

Dual Hydraulic Braking System A brake system consisting of a tandem, or double action master cylinder which is basically two master cylinders usually formed by aligning two separate pistons and fluid reservoirs into a single cylinder.

ECU An abbreviation for electronic control unit.

Eddy Current A small circular current produced inside a metal core in the armature of a starter motor. Eddy currents produce heat and are reduced by using a laminated core.

Electricity The movement of electrons from one place to another.

Electric Retarder Electromagnets mounted in a steel frame. Energizing the retarder causes the electromagnets to exert a dragging force on the rotors in the frame and this drag force is transmitted directly to the drive shaft.

Electromotive Force (EMF) The force that moves electrons between atoms. This force is the pressure that exists between the positive and negative points (the electrical imbalance). This force is measured in units called volts.

Electronically Programmable Memory (EPROM) Computer memory that permits adaptation of the ECU to various standard mechanically controlled functions.

Electronic Control Unit (ECU) The brain of the vehicle.

Electronics The technology of controlling electricity.

Electrons Negatively charged particles orbiting around every nucleus.

Elliot Axle A solid bar front axle on which the ends span the steering knuckle.

EMF An abbreviation for electromotive force.

End Yoke The component connected to the output shaft of the transmission to transfer engine torque to the drive shaft.

Engine Brake A hydraulically operated device that converts the vehicle's engine into a power absorbing retarding mechanism.

Engine Stall Point The point, in rpms, under load is compared to the engine manufacturer's specified rpm for the stall test.

Environmental Protection Agency An agency of the United States government charged with the responsibilities of protecting the environment and enforcing the Clean Air Act (CAA) of 1990.

EPA An abbreviation for the Environmental Protection Agency.

EPROM An abbreviation for Electronically Programmable Memory.

Equalizer A suspension device used to transfer and maintain equal load distribution between two or more axles of a suspension. Formerly called a rocker beam.

Equalizer Bracket A bracket for mounting the equalizer beam of a multiple axle spring suspension to a truck or trailer frame while allowing for the beam's pivotal movement. Normally there are three basic types: flange-mount, straddle-mount, and under- or side-mount.

Evaporator A component in an air conditioning system used to remove heat from the air passing through it.

Exhaust Brake A valve in the exhaust pipe between the manifold and the muffler. A slide mechanism which restricts the exhaust flow, causing exhaust back pressure to build up in the engine's cylinders. The exhaust brake actually transforms the engine into a low pressure air compressor driven by the wheels.

External Housing Damper A counterweight attached to an arm on the rear of the transmission extension housing and designed to dampen unwanted driveline or powertrain vibrations.

Extra Capacity A term that generally refers to: (1) A coupling device that has strength capability greater than standard. (2) An oversized tank or reservoir for a fluid or vapor.

False Brinelling The polishing of a surface that is not damaged.

Fanning the Brakes Applying and releasing the brakes in rapid succession on a long downgrade.

Fatigue Failures The progressive destruction of a shaft or gear teeth material usually caused by overloading.

Fault Code A code that is recorded into the computer's memory. A fault code can be read by plugging a special break-out box tester into the computer.

Federal Motor Vehicle Safety Standard (FMVSS) A federal standard that specifies that all vehicles in the United States be assigned a Vehicle Identification Number (VIN).

Federal Motor Vehicle Safety Standard No. 121 (FMVSS 121) A federal standard that made significant changes in the guidelines that cover air brake systems. Generally speaking, the requirements of FMVSS 121 are such that larger capacity brakes and heavier steerable axles are needed to meet them.

FHWA An abbreviation for Federal Highway Administration.

Fiber Composite Springs Springs that are made of fiberglass, laminated, and bonded together by tough polyester resins.

Fifth Wheel A coupling device mounted on a truck and used to connect a semitrailer. It acts as a hinge point to allow changes in direction of travel between the tractor and the semitrailer.

Fifth Wheel Height The distance from the ground to the top of the fifth wheel when it is level and parallel with the ground. It can also refer to the height from the tractor frame to the top of the fifth wheel. The latter definition applies to data given in fifth wheel literature.

Fifth Wheel Top Plate The portion of the fifth wheel assembly that contacts the trailer bolster plate and houses the locking mechanism that connects to the kingpin.

Final Drive The last reduction gear set of a truck.

Fixed Value Resistor An electrical device that is designed to have only one resistance rating, which should not change, for controlling voltage.

Flammable Any material that will easily catch fire or explode.

Flare To spread gradually outward in a bell shape.

Flex Disc A term often used for flex plate.

Flex Plate A component used to mount the torque converter to the crankshaft. The flex plate is positioned between the engine crankshaft and the T/C. The purpose of the flex plate is to transfer crankshaft rotation to the shell of the torque converter assembly.

Float A cruising drive mode in which the throttle setting matches engine speed to road speed, neither accelerating nor decelerating.

Floating Main Shaft The main shaft consisting of a heavy-duty central shaft and several gears that turn freely when not engaged. The main shaft can move to allow for equalization of the loading on the countershafts. This is key to making a twin countershaft transmission workable. When engaged, the floating main shaft transfers torque evenly through its gears to the rest of the transmission and ultimately to the rear axle.

FMVSS An abbreviation for Federal Motor Vehicle Safety Standard.

FMVSS No 121 An abbreviation for Federal Motor Vehicle Safety Standard No 121.

Foot Valve A foot-operated brake valve that controls air pressure to the service chambers.

Foot-Pound An English unit of measurement for torque. One foot-pound is the torque obtained by a force of 1 pound applied to a foot long wrench handle.

Forged Journal Cross Part of a universal joint.

Frame Width The measurement across the outside of the frame rails of a tractor, truck, or trailer.

Franchised Dealership A dealer that has signed a contract with a particular manufacturer to sell and service a particular line of vehicles.

Fretting A result of vibration that the bearing outer race can pick up the machining pattern.

Friction Plate Assembly An assembly consisting of a multiple disc clutch that is designed to slip when a predetermined torque value is reached.

Front Axle Limiting Valve A valve that reduces pressure to the front service chambers, thus eliminating front wheel lockup on wet or icy pavements.

Front Hanger A bracket for mounting the front of the truck or trailer suspensions to the frame. Made to accommodate the end of the spring on spring suspensions. There are four basic types: flange-mount, straddle-mount, under-mount, and side-mount.

Full Trailer A trailer that does not transfer load to the towing vehicle. It employs a tow bar coupled to a swiveling or steerable running gear assembly at the front of the trailer.

Fully Floating Axles An axle configuration whereby the axle half shafts transmit only driving torque to the wheels and not bending and torsional loads that are characteristic of the semi-floating axle.

Fully Oscillating Fifth Wheel A fifth wheel type with fore/aft and side-to-side articulation.

Fusible Link A term often used for fuse link.

Fuse Link A short length of smaller gauge wire installed in a conductor, usually close to the power source.

GCW An abbreviation for gross combination weight.

Gear A disk-like wheel with external or internal teeth that serves to transmit or change motion.

Gear Pitch The number of teeth per given unit of pitch diameter, an important factor in gear design and operation.

General Over-the-Road Use A fifth wheel designed for multiple standard duty highway applications.

Gladhand The connectors between tractor and trailer air lines.

Gross Combination Weight (GCW) The total weight of a fully quipped vehicle including payload, fuel, and driver.

Gross Trailer Weight (GTW) The sum of the weight of an empty trailer and its payload.

Gross Vehicle Weight (GVW) The total weight of a fully equipped vehicle and its payload.

Ground The negatively charged side of a circuit. A ground can be a wire, the negative side of the battery, or the vehicle chassis.

Grounded Circuit A shorted circuit that causes current to return to the battery before it has reached its intended destination.

GTW An abbreviation for gross trailer weight.

GVW An abbreviation for gross vehicle weight.

Halogen Light A lamp having a small quartz/glass bulb that contains a fuel filament surrounded by halogen gas. It is contained within a larger metal reflector and lens element.

Hand Valve (1) A valve mounted on the steering column or dash, used by the driver to apply the trailer brakes independently of the tractor brakes. (2) A hand operated valve used to control the flow of fluid or vapor.

Harness and Harness Connectors The organization of the vehicle's electrical system providing an orderly and convenient starting point for tracking and testing circuits.

Hazardous Materials Any substance that is flammable, explosive, or is known to produce adverse health effects in people or the environment that are exposed to the material during its use.

Heads Up Display (HUD) A technology used in some vehicles that superimposes data on the driver's normal field of vision. The operator can view the information, which appears to "float" just above the hood at a range near the front of a conventional tractor or truck. This allows the driver to monitor conditions such as limited road speed without interrupting his normal view of traffic.

Heater Control Valve A valve that controls the flow of coolant into the heater core from the engine.

Heat Exchanger A device used to transfer heat, such as a radiator or condenser.

Heavy-Duty Truck A truck that has a GVW of 26,001 pounds or more.

Helper Spring An additional spring device that permits greater load on an axle.

High CG Load Any application in which the load center of gravity (CG) of the trailer exceeds 40 inches (102 centimeters) above the top of the fifth wheel.

High-Resistant Circuits Circuits that have an increase in circuit resistance, with a corresponding decrease in current.

High-Strength Steel A low-alloy steel that is much stronger than hot-rolled or cold-rolled sheet steels that normally are used in the manufacture of car body frames.

Hinged Pawl Switch The simplest type of switch; one that makes or breaks the current of a single conductor.

HUD An abbreviation for heads up display.

Hydraulic Brakes Brakes that are actuated by a hydraulic system.

Hydraulic Brake System A system utilizing the properties of fluids under pressure to activate the brakes.

Hydrometer A tester designed to measure the specific gravity of a liquid.

Hypoid Gears Gears that intersect at right angles when meshed. Hypoid gearing uses a modified spiral bevel gear structure that allows several gear teeth to absorb the driving power and allows the gears to run quietly. A hypoid gear is typically found at the drive pinion gear and ring gear interface.

I-Beam Axle An axle designed to give great strength at reasonable weight. The cross section of the axle resembles the letter "I."

ICC Check Valve A valve that allows air to flow in one direction only. It is a federal requirement to have a check valve between the wet and dry air tanks.

Inboard Toward the centerline of the vehicle.

In-Line Fuse A fuse that is in series with the circuit in a small plastic fuse holder, not in the fuse box or panel. It is used, when necessary, as a protection device for a portion of the circuit even though the entire circuit may be protected by a fuse in the fuse box or panel.

In-Phase The in-line relationship between the forward coupling shaft yoke and the driveshaft slip yoke of a two-piece drive line.

Input Retarder A device located between the torque converter housing and the main housing designed primarily for over-the-road operations. The device employs a "paddle wheel" type design with a vaned rotor mounted between stator vanes in the retarder housing.

Installation Templates Drawings supplied by some vehicle manufacturers to allow the technician to correctly install the accessory. The templates available can be used to check clearances or to ease installation.

Insulator A material, such as rubber or glass, that offers high resistance to the flow of electrons.

Integrated Circuit A component containing diodes, transistors, resistors, capacitors, and other electronic components mounted on a single piece of material and capable to perform numerous functions.

Jacobs Engine Brake A term sometimes used for Jake brake.

Jake Brake The Jacobs engine brake, named for its inventor. A hydraulically operated device that converts a power producing diesel engine into a power-absorbing retarder mechanism by altering the engine's exhaust valve opening time used to slow the vehicle.

Jumper Wire A wire used to temporarily bypass a circuit or components for electrical testing. A jumper wire consists of a length of wire with an alligator clip at each end.

Jumpout A condition that occurs when a fully engaged gear and sliding clutch are forced out of engagement.

Jump Start The procedure used when it becomes necessary to use a booster battery to start a vehicle having a discharged battery.

Kinetic Energy Energy in motion.

Kingpin (1) The pin mounted through the center of the trailer upper coupler (bolster plate) that mates with the fifth wheel locks, securing the trailer to the fifth wheel. The configuration is controlled by industry standards. (2) A pin or shaft on which the steering spindle rotates.

Landing Gear The retractable supports for a semitrailer to keep the trailer level when the tractor is detached from it.

Lateral Runout The wobble or side-to-side movement of a rotating wheel or of a rotating wheel and tire assembly.

Lazer Beam Alignment System A two- or four-wheel alignment system using wheel-mounted instruments to project a lazer beam to measure toe, caster, and camber.

Lead The tendency of a car to deviate from a straight path on a level road when there is no pressure on the steering wheel in either direction.

Leaf Springs Strips of steel connected to the chassis and axle to isolate the vehicle from road shock.

Less Than Truckload (LTL) Partial loads from the networks of consolidation centers and satellite terminals.

Light Beam Alignment System An alignment system using wheel-mounted instruments to project light beams onto charts and scales to measure toe, caster, and camber, and note the results of alignment adjustments.

Limited-Slip Differential A differential that utilizes a clutch device to deliver power to either rear wheel when the opposite wheel is spinning.

Linkage A system of rods and levers used to transmit motion or force.

Live Axle An axle on which the wheels are firmly affixed. The axle drives the wheels.

Live Beam Axle A non-independent suspension in which the axle moves with the wheels.

Load Proportioning Valve (LPV) A valve used to redistribute hydraulic pressure to front and rear brakes based on vehicle loads. This is a load- or height-sensing valve that senses the vehicle load and proportions the braking between front and rear brakes in proportion to the load variations and degree of rear-to-front weight transfer during braking.

Lockstrap A manual adjustment mechanism that allows for the adjustment of free travel.

Lock-up Torque Converter A torque converter that eliminates the 10 percent slip that takes place between the impeller and turbine at the coupling stage of operation. It is considered a four-element (impeller, turbine, stator, lockup clutch), three-stage (stall, coupling, and locking stage) unit.

Longitudinal Leaf Spring A leaf spring that is mounted so it is parallel to the length of the vehicle.

Low-Maintenance Battery A conventionally vented, lead/acid battery, requiring normal periodic maintenance.

LTL An abbreviation for less than truckload.

Magnetorque An electromagnetic clutch.

Maintenance-Free Battery A battery that does not require the addition of water during normal service life.

Maintenance Manual A publication containing routine maintenance procedures and intervals for vehicle components and systems.

Main Transmission A transmission consisting of an input shaft, floating main shaft assembly and main drive gears, two counter shaft assemblies, and reverse idler gears.

Manual Slide Release The release mechanism for a sliding fifth wheel, which is operated by hand.

Metering Valve A valve used on vehicles equipped with front disc and rear drum brakes. It improves braking balance during light brake applications by preventing application of the front disc brakes until pressure is built up in the hydraulic system.

Moisture Ejector A valve mounted to the bottom or side of the supply and service reservoirs that collects water and expels it every time the air pressure fluctuates.

Mounting Bracket That portion of the fifth wheel assembly that connects the fifth wheel top plate to the tractor frame or fifth wheel mounting system.

Multiaxle Suspension A suspension consisting of more than three axles.

Multiple Disc Clutch A clutch having a large drum-shaped housing that can be either a separate casting or part of the existing transmission housing.

NATEF An abbreviation for National Automotive Education Foundation.

National Automotive Education Foundation (NATEF) A foundation having a program of certifying secondary and post secondary automotive and heavy-duty truck training programs.

National Institute for Automotive Service Excellence (ASE) A nonprofit organization that has an established certification program for automotive, heavy-duty truck, auto body repair, engine machine shop technicians, and parts specialists.

Needlenose Pliers This tool has long tapered jaws for grasping small parts or for reaching into tight spots. Many needlenose pliers also have cutting edges and a wire stripper.

NIASE An abbreviation for National Institute for Automotive Service Excellence, now abbreviated ASE.

NIOSH An abbreviation for National Institute for Occupation Safety and Health.

NLGI An abbreviation for National Lubricating Grease Institute.

NHTSA An abbreviation for National Highway Traffic Safety Administration.

Nonlive Axle Non-live or dead axles are often mounted in lifting suspensions. They hold the axle off the road when the vehicle is traveling empty, and put it on the road when a load is being carried. They are also used as air suspension third axles on heavy straight trucks and are used extensively in eastern states with high axle weight laws.

Nonparallel Driveshaft A type of drive shaft installation whereby the working angles of the joints of a given shaft are equal; however the companion flanges and/or yokes are not parallel.

Nonpolarized Gladhand A gladhand that can be connected to either service or emergency gladhand.

Nose The front of a semitrailer.

No-tilt Convertible Fifth A fifth wheel with fore/aft articulation that can be locked out to produce a rigid top plate for applications that have either rigid and/or articulating upper couplers.

(OEM) An abbreviation for original equipment manufacturer.

Off-road With reference to unpaved, rough, or ungraded terrain on which a vehicle will operate. Any terrain not considered part of the highway system falls into this category.

Ohm A unit of measured electrical resistance.

Ohm's Law The basic law of electricity stating that in any electrical circuit, current, resistance, and pressure work together in a mathematical relationship.

On-road With reference to paved or smooth-graded surface terrain on which a vehicle will operate, generally considered to be part of the public highway system.

Open Circuit An electrical circuit whose path has been interrupted or broken either accidentally (a broken wire) or intentionally (a switch turned off).

Operational Control Valve A valve used to control the flow of compressed air through the brake system.

Oscillation The rotational movement in either fore/aft or side-to-side direction about a pivot point. Generally refers to fifth wheel designs in which fore/aft and side-to-side articulation are provided.

OSHA An abbreviation for Occupational Safety and Health Administration.

Out-of-Phase A condition of the universal joint which acts somewhat like one person snapping a rope held by a person at the opposite end. The result is a violent reaction at the opposite end. If both were to snap the rope at the same time, the resulting waves cancel each other and neither would feel the reaction.

Out-of-Round A wheel or tire defect in which the wheel or tire is not round.

Output Driver An electronic on/off switch that the computer uses to control the ground circuit of a specific actuator. Output drivers are located in the processor along with the input conditioners, microprocessor, and memory.

Output Yoke The component that serves as a connecting link, transferring torque from the transmission's output shaft through the vehicle's drive line to the rear axle.

Oval A condition that occurs when a tube is not round, but is somewhat egg-shaped.

Overall Ratio The ratio of the lowest to the highest forward gear in the transmission.

Overdrive The gearing of a transmission so that in its highest gear one revolution of the engine produces more than one revolution of the transmission's output shaft.

Overrunning Clutch A clutch mechanism that transmits power in one direction only.

Overspeed Governor A governor that shuts off the fuel or stops the engine when excessive speed is reached.

Oxidation Inhibitor (1) An additive used with lubricating oils to keep oil from oxidizing even at very high temperatures. (2) An additive for gasoline to reduce the chemicals in gasoline that react with oxygen.

Pad A disc brake lining and metal back riveted, molded, or bonded together.

Parallel Circuit An electrical circuit that provides two or more paths for the current to flow. Each path has separate resistors and operates independently from the other parallel paths. In a parallel circuit, amperage can flow through more than one resistor at a time.

Parallel Joint Type A type of drive shaft installation whereby all companion flanges and/or yokes in the complete drive line are parallel to each other with the working angles of the joints of a given shaft being equal and opposite.

Parking Brake A mechanically applied brake used to prevent a parked vehicle's movement.

Parts Requisition A form that is used to order new parts, on which the technician writes the names of what part(s) are needed along with the vehicle's VIN or company's identification folder.

Payload The weight of the cargo carried by a truck, not including the weight of the body.

Pipe or Angle Brace Extrusions between opposite hangers on a spring or air-type suspension.

Pitman Arm A steering linkage component that connects the steering gear to the linkage at the left end of the center link.

Pitting Surface irregularities resulting from corrosion.

Planetary Drive A planetary gear reduction set where the sun gear is the drive and the planetary carrier is the output.

Planetary Gear Set A system of gearing that is somewhat like the solar system. A pinion is surrounded by an internal ring gear and planet

gears are in mesh between the ring gear and pinion around which all revolve.

Planetary Pinion Gears Small gears fitted into a framework called the planetary carrier.

Plies The layers of rubber-impregnated fabric that make up the body of a tire.

Pogo Stick The air and electrical line support rod mounted behind the cab to keep the lines from dragging between the tractor and trailer.

Polarity The particular state, either positive or negative, with reference to the two poles or to electrification.

Pole The number of input circuits made by an electrical switch.

Pounds per Square Inch (psi) A unit of English measure for pressure.

Power A measure of work being done.

Power Flow The flow of power from the input shaft through one or more sets of gears, or through an automatic transmission to the output shaft.

Power Steering A steering system utilizing hydraulic pressure to reduce the turning effort required of the operator.

Power Synchronizer A device to speed up the rotation of the main section gearing for smoother automatic downshifts and to slow down the rotation of the main section gearing for smoother automatic upshifts.

Power Train An assembly consisting of a drive shaft, coupling, clutch, and transmission differential.

Pressure The amount of force applied to a definite area measured in pounds per square inch (psi) English or kilopascals (kPa) metric.

Pressure Differential The difference in pressure between any two points of a system or a component.

Pressure Relief Valve (1) A valve located on the wet tank, usually preset at 150 psi (1,034 kPa). Limits system pressure if the compressor or governor unloader valve malfunctions. (2) A valve located on the rear head of an air-conditioning compressor or pressure vessel that opens if an excessive system pressure is exceeded.

Printed Circuit Board An electronic circuit board made of thin nonconductive plastic-like material onto which conductive metal, such as copper, has been deposited. Parts of the metal are then etched away by an acid, leaving metal lines that form the conductors for the various circuits on the board. A printed circuit board can hold many complex circuits in a very small area.

Programmable Read Only Memory (PROM) An electronic component that contains program information specific to different vehicle model calibrations.

PROM An abbreviation for Programmable Read Only Memory.

Priority Valve A valve that ensures that the control system upstream from the valve will have sufficient pressure during shifts to perform its automatic functions.

Proportioning Valve A valve used on vehicles equipped with front disc and rear drum brakes. It is installed in the lines to the rear drum brakes, and in a split system, below the pressure differential valve. By reducing pressure to the rear drum brakes, the valve helps to prevent premature lockup during severe brake application and provides better braking balance.

Psi An abbreviation for pounds per square inch.

Pull Circuit A circuit that brings the cab from a fully tilted position up and over the center.

Pull-Type Clutch A type of clutch that does not push the release bearing toward the engine; instead, it pulls the release bearing toward the transmission.

Pump/Impeller Assembly The input (drive) member that receives power from the engine.

Push Circuit A circuit that raises the cab from the lowered position to the desired tilt position.

Push-Type Clutch A type of clutch in which the release bearing is not attached to the clutch cover.

P-type Semiconductors Positively charged materials that enables them to carry current. They are produced by adding an impurity with three electrons in the outer ring (trivalent atoms).

Quick Release Valve A device used to exhaust air as close as possible to the service chambers or spring brakes.

Radial A tire design having cord materials running in a direction from the center point of the tire, usually from bead to bead.

Radial Load A load that is applied at 90° to an axis of rotation.

RAM An abbreviation for random access memory.

Ram Air Air that is forced into the engine or passenger compartment by the forward motion of the vehicle.

Random Access Memory (RAM) The memory used during computer operation to store temporary information. The microcomputer can write, read, and erase information from RAM in any order, which is why it is called random.

Range Shift Cylinder A component located in the auxiliary section of the transmission. This component, when directed by air pressure via low and high ports, shifts between high and low range of gears.

Range Shift Lever A lever located on the shift knob allows the driver to select low or high gear range.

Rated Capacity The maximum, recommended safe load that can be sustained by a component or an assembly without permanent damage.

Ratio Valve A valve used on the front or steering axle of a heavy-duty truck to limit the brake application pressure to the actuators during normal service braking.

RCRA An abbreviation for Resource Conservation and Recovery Act.

Reactivity The characteristic of a material that enables it to react violently with air, heat, water, or other materials.

Read Only Memory (ROM) A type of memory used in microcomputers to store information permanently.

Rear Hanger A bracket for mounting the rear of a truck or trailer suspension to the frame. Made to accommodate the end of the spring on spring suspensions. There are usually four types: flange-mount, straddle-mount, under-mount, and side-mount.

Recall Bulletin A bulletin that pertains to special situations that involve service work or replacement of parts in connection with a recall notice.

Reference Voltage The voltage supplied to a sensor by the computer, which acts as a base line voltage; modified by the sensor to act as an input signal.

Relay An electric switch that allows a small current to control a much larger one. It consists of a control circuit and a power circuit.

Relay/Quick Release Valve A valve used on trucks with a wheel base 254 inches (6.45 meters) or longer. It is attached to an air tank to main supply line to speed the application and release of air to the service chambers. It is similar to a remote control foot valve.

Refrigerant A liquid capable of vaporizing at a low temperature.

Refrigerant Management Center Equipment designed to recover, recycle, and recharge an air-conditioning system.

Release Bearing A unit within the clutch consisting of bearings that mount on the transmission input shaft but do not rotate with it.

Reserve Capacity Rating The ability of a battery to sustain a minimum vehicle electrical load in the event of a charging system failure.

Resistance The opposition to current flow in an electrical circuit.

Resisting Bending Moment A measurement of frame rail strength derived by multiplying the section modulus of the rail by the yield strength of the material. This term is universally used in evaluating frame rail strength.

Resource Conservation and Recovery Act (RCRA) A law that states that after using a hazardous material, it must be properly stored until an approved hazardous waste hauler arrives to take them to the disposal site.

Reverse Elliot Axle A solid-beam front axle on which the steering knuckles span the axle ends.

Revolutions per Minute (rpm) The number of complete turns a member makes in one minute.

Right to Know Law A law passed by the federal government and administered by the Occupational Safety and Health Administration (OSHA) that requires any company that uses or produces hazardous chemicals or substances to inform its employees, customers, and vendors of any potential hazards that may exist in the workplace as a result of using the products.

Rigid Disc A steel plate to which friction linings, or facings, are bonded or riveted.

Rigid Fifth Wheel A platform that is fixed rigidly to a frame. This fifth wheel has no articulation or oscillation. It is generally used in applications where the articulation is provided by other means, such as an articulating upper coupler of a frame-less dump.

Rigid Torque Arm A member used to retain axle alignment and, in some cases, to control axle torque. Normally, one adjustable and one rigid arm are used per axle so the axle can be aligned.

Ring Gear (1) The gear around the edge of a flywheel. (2) A large circular gear such as that found in a final drive assembly.

Rocker Beam A suspension device used to transfer and maintain equal load distribution between two or more axles of a suspension.

Roll Axis The theoretical line that joins the roll center of the front and rear axles.

Roller Clutch A clutch designed with a movable inner race, rollers, accordion (apply) springs, and outer race. Around the inside diameter of the outer race are several cam-shaped pockets. The clutch assembly rollers and accordion springs are located in these pockets.

Rollers A hardware part that attaches to the web of the brake shoes by means of roller retainers. The rollers, in turn, ride on the end of an S-cam.

ROM An abbreviation for read only memory.

Rotary Oil Flow A condition caused by the centrifugal force applied to the fluid as the converter rotates around its axis.

Rotation A term used to describe the fact that a gear, shaft, or other device is turning.

rpm An abbreviation for revolutions per minute.

Rotor (1) A part of the alternator that provides the magnetic fields necessary to create a current flow. (2) The rotating member of an assembly.

Runout A deviation of the specified normal travel of an object. The amount of deviation or wobble a shaft or wheel has as it rotates. Runout is measured with a dial indicator.

Safety Factor (SF) (1) The amount of load which can safely be absorbed by and through the vehicle chassis frame members. (2) The difference between the stated and rated limits of a product, such as a grinding disk.

Screw Pitch Gauge A gauge used to provide a quick and accurate method of checking the threads per inch of a nut or bolt.

Secondary Lock The component or components of a fifth wheel locking mechanism that can be included as a backup system for the primary locks. The secondary lock is not required for the fifth wheel to function and can be either manually or automatically applied. On some designs, the engagement of the secondary lock can only be accomplished if the primary lock is properly engaged.

Section Height The tread center to bead plane on a tire.

Section Width The measurement on a tire from sidewall to sidewall.

Self-Adjusting Clutch A clutch that automatically takes up the slack between the pressure plate and clutch disc as wear occurs.

Semiconductor A solid state device that can function as either a conductor or an insulator, depending on how its structure is arranged.

Semifloating Axle An axle type whereby drive power from the differential is taken by each axle half-shaft and transferred directly to the wheels. A single bearing assembly, located at the outer end of the axle, is used to support the axle half-shaft.

Semioscillating A term that generally describes a fifth wheel type that oscillates or articulates about an axis perpendicular to the vehicle centerline.

Semitrailer A load-carrying vehicle equipped with one or more axles and constructed so that its front end is supported on the fifth wheel of the truck tractor that pulls it.

Sensing Voltage The voltage that allows the regulator to sense and monitor the battery voltage level.

Sensor An electronic device used to monitor relative conditions for computer control requirements.

Series Circuit A circuit that consists of two or more resistors connected to a voltage source with only one path for the electrons to follow.

Series/Parallel Circuit A circuit designed so that both series and parallel combinations exist within the same circuit.

Service Bulletin A publication that provides the latest service tips, field repairs, product improvements, and related information of benefit to service personnel.

Service Manual A manual, published by the manufacturer, that contains service and repair information for all vehicle systems and components.

Shift Bar Housing Available in standard- and forward-position configurations, a component that houses the shift rails, shift yokes, detent balls and springs, inter-lock balls, and pin and neutral shaft.

Shift Fork The Y-shaped component located between the gears on the main shaft that, when actuated, cause the gears to engage or disengage via the sliding clutches. Shift forks are located between low and reverse, first and second, and third and fourth gears.

Shift Rail Shift rails guide the shift forks using a series of grooves, tension balls, and springs to hold the shift forks in gear. The grooves in the forks allow them to interlock the rails, and the transmission cannot be accidentally shifted into two gears at the same time.

Shift Tower The main interface between the driver and the transmission, consisting of a gearshift lever, pivot pin, spring, boot and housing.

Shift Yoke A Y-shaped component located between the gears on the main shaft that, when actuated, cause the gears to engage or disengage via the sliding clutches. Shift yokes are located between low and reverse, first and second, and third and fourth gears.

Shock Absorber A hydraulic device used to dampen vehicle spring oscillations for controlling body sway and wheel bounce, and/or prevent spring breakage.

Short Circuit An undesirable connection between two worn or damaged wires. The short occurs when the insulation is worn between two adjacent wires and the metal in each wire contacts the other, or when the wires are damaged or pinched.

Single-Axle Suspension A suspension with one axle.

Single Reduction Axle Any axle assembly that employs only one gear reduction through its differential carrier assembly.

Slave Valve A valve to help protect gears and components in the transmission's auxiliary section by permitting range shifts to occur only when the transmission's main gearbox is in neutral. Air pressure from a regulator signals the slave valve into operation.

Slide Travel The distance that a sliding fifth wheel is designed to move.

Sliding Fifth Wheel A specialized fifth wheel design that incorporates provisions to readily relocate the kingpin center forward and rearward, which affects the weight distribution on the tractor axles and/or overall length of the tractor and trailer.

Slipout A condition that generally occurs when pulling with full power or decelerating with the load pushing. Tapered or worn clutching teeth will try to "walk" apart as the gears rotate, causing the sliding clutch and gear to slip out of engagement.

Slip Rings and Brushes Components of an alternator that conducts current to the rotor. Most alternators have two slip rings mounted directly on the rotor shaft; they are insulated from the shaft and from each other. A spring loaded carbon brush is located on each slip ring to carry the current to and from the rotor windings.

Solenoid An electromagnet that is used to perform work, made with one or two coil windings wound around an iron tube.

Solid-State Device A device that requires very little power to operate, is very reliable, and generates very little heat.

Solid Wires A single-strand conductor.

Solvent A substance which dissolves other substances.

Spade Fuse A term used for blade fuse.

Spalling Surface fatigue occurs when chips, scales, or flakes of metal break off due to fatigue rather than wear. Spalling is usually found on splines and U-joint bearings.

Specialty Service Shop A shop that specializes in areas such as engine rebuilding, transmission/axle overhauling, brake, air conditioning/heating repairs, and electrical/electronic work.

Specific Gravity The scientific measurement of a liquid based on the ratio of the liquid's mass to an equal volume of distilled water.

Spiral Bevel Gear A gear arrangement that has a drive pinion gear that meshes with the ring gear at the centerline axis of the ring gear. This gearing provides strength and allows for quiet operation.

Splined Yoke A yoke that allows the drive shaft to increase in length to accommodate movements of the drive axles.

Spontaneous Combustion A process by which a combustible material ignites by itself and starts a fire.

Spread Tandem Suspension A two-axle assembly in which the axles are spaced to allow maximum axle loads under existing regulations. The distance is usually more than 55 inches.

Spring A device used to reduce road shocks and transfer loads through suspension components to the frame of the trailer. There are usually four basic types: multileaf, monoleaf, taper, and air springs.

Spring Chair A suspension component used to support and locate the spring on an axle.

Spring Deflection The depression of a trailer suspension when the springs are placed under load.

Spring Rate The load required to deflect the spring a given distance, (usually one inch).

Spring Spacer A riser block often used on top of the spring seat to obtain increased mounting height.

Stability A relative measure of the handling characteristics which provide the desired and safe operation of the vehicle during various maneuvers.

Stabilizer A device used to stabilize a vehicle during turns; sometimes referred to as a sway bar.

Stabilizer Bar A bar that connects the two sides of a suspension so that cornering forces on one wheel are shaped by the other. This helps equalize wheel side loading and reduces the tendency of the vehicle body to roll outward in a turn.

Staff Test A test performed when there is an obvious malfunction in the vehicle's power package (engine and transmission), to determine which of the components is at fault.

Stand Pipe A type of check valve which prevents reverse flow of the hot liquid lubricant generated during operation. When the universal joint is at rest, one or more of the cross ends will be up. Without the stand pipe, lubricant would flow out of the upper passage ways and trunnions, leading to partially dry startup.

Starter Circuit The circuit that carries the high current flow within the system and supplies power for the actual engine cranking.

Starter Motor The device that converts the electrical energy from the battery into mechanical energy for cranking the engine.

Starting Safety Switch A switch that prevents vehicles with automatic transmissions from being started in gear.

Static Balance Balance at rest, or still balance. It is the equal distribution of the weight of the wheel and tire around the axis of rotation so that the wheel assembly has no tendency to rotate by itself regardless of its position.

Stationary Fifth Wheel A fifth wheel whose location on the tractor frame is fixed once it is installed.

Stator A component located between the pump/impeller and turbine to redirect the oil flow from the turbine back into the impeller in the direction of impeller rotation with minimal loss of speed or force.

Stator Assembly The reaction member or torque multiplier supported on a free wheel roller race that is splined to the valve and front support assembly.

Steering Gear A gear set mounted in a housing that is fastened to the lower end of the steering column used to multiply driver turning force and change rotary motion into longitudinal motion.

Steering Stabilizer A shock absorber attached to the steering components to cushion road shock in the steering system, improving driver control in rough terrain and protecting the system.

Stepped Resistor A resistor designed to have two or more fixed values, available by connecting wires to either of the several taps.

Still Balance Balance at rest; the equal distribution of the weight of the wheel and tire around the axis of rotation so that the wheel assembly has no tendency to rotate by itself regardless of its position.

Stoplight Switch A pneumatic switch that actuates the brake lights. There are two types: (1) A service stoplight switch that is located in the service circuit, actuated when the service brakes are applied. (2) An emergency stoplight switch located in the emergency circuit and actuated when a pressure loss occurs.

Storage Battery A battery to provide a source of direct current electricity for both the electrical and electronic systems.

Stranded Wire Wire that is are made up of a number of small solid wires, generally twisted together, to form a single conductor.

Structural Member A primary load-bearing portion of the body structure that affects its over-the-road performance or crash-worthiness.

Sulfation A condition that occurs when sulfate is allowed to remain in the battery plates for a long time, causing two problems: (1) It lowers the specific gravity levels, increasing the danger of freezing at low temperatures. (2) In cold weather a sulfated battery may not have the reserve power needed to crank the engine.

Suspension A system whereby the axle or axles of a unit are attached to the vehicle frame, designed in such a manner that road shocks from the axles are dampened through springs reducing the forces entering the frame.

Suspension Height The distance from a specified point on a vehicle to the road surface when not at curb weight.

Swage To reduce or taper.

Sway Bar A component that connects the two sides of a suspension so that cornering forces on one wheel are shared by the other. This helps equalize wheel side loading and reduces the tendency of the vehicle body to roll outward in a turn.

Switch A device used to control on/off and direct the flow of current in a circuit. A switch can be under the control of the driver or can be self-operating through a condition of the circuit, the vehicle, or the environment.

Synchromesh A mechanism that equalizes the speed of the gears that are clutched together.

Synchro-transmission A transmission with mechanisms for synchronizing the gear speeds so that the gears can be shifted without clashing, thus eliminating the need for double-clutching.

System Protection Valve A valve to protect the brake system against an accidental loss of air pressure, buildup of excess pressure, or back-flow and reverse air flow.

Tachometer An instrument that indicates rotating speeds, sometimes used to indicate crankshaft rpm.

Tag Axle The rearmost axle of a tandem axle tractor used to increase the load-carrying capacity of the vehicle.

Tapped Resistor A resistor designed to have two or more fixed values, available by connecting wires to either of the several taps.

Tandem One directly in front of the other and working together.

Tandem Axle Suspension A suspension system consisting of two axles with a means for equalizing weight between them.

Tandem Drive A two-axle drive combination.

Tandem Drive Axle A type of axle that combines two single axle assemblies through the use of an interaxle differential or power divider and a short shaft that connects the two axles together.

Three-Speed Differential A type of axle in a tandem two-speed axle arrangement with the capability of operating the two drive axles in different speed ranges at the same time. The third speed is actually an intermediate speed between the high and low range.

Throw (1) The offset of a crankshaft. (2) The number of output circuits of a switch.

Tie-Rod Assembly A system that transfers the steering motion to the opposite, passenger side steering knuckle. It links the two steering knuckles together and forces them to act in unison.

Time Guide Prepared reference material used for computing compensation payable by the truck manufacturer for repairs or service work to vehicles under warranty, or for other special conditions authorized by the company.

Timing (1) A procedure of marking the appropriate teeth of a gear set prior to installation and placing them in proper mesh while in the transmission. (2) The combustion spark delivery in relation to the piston position.

Toe A suspension dimension that reflects the difference in the distance between the extreme front and rear of the tire.

Toe In A suspension dimension whereby the front of the tire points inward toward the vehicle.

Toe Out A suspension dimension whereby the front of the tire points outward from the vehicle.

Top U-Bolt Plate A plate located on the top of the spring and is held in place when the U-bolts are tightened to clamp the spring and axle together.

Torque To tighten a fastener to a specific degree of tightness, generally in a given order or pattern if multiple fasteners are involved on a single component.

Torque and Twist A term that generally refers to the forces developed in the trailer and/or tractor frame that are transmitted through the fifth wheel when a rigid trailer, such as a tanker, is required to negotiate bumps, like street curbs.

Torque Converter A component device, similar to a fluid coupling, that transfers engine torque to the transmission input shaft and can multiply engine torque by having one or more stators between the members.

Torque Limiting Clutch Brake A system designed to slip when loads of 20 to 25 pound–feet (27 to 34 N) are reached protecting the brake from overloading and the resulting high heat damage.

Torque Rod Shim A thin wedge-like insert that rotates the axle pinion to change the U-joint operating angle.

Torsional Rigidity A component's ability to remain rigid when subjected to twisting forces.

Torsion Bar Suspension A type of suspension system that utilizes torsion bars in lieu of steel leaf springs or coil springs. The typical torsion bar suspension consists of a torsion bar, front crank, and rear crank with associated brackets, a shackle pin, and assorted bushings and seals.

Total Pedal Travel The complete distance the clutch or brake pedal must move.

Toxicity A statement of how poisonous a substance is.

Tracking The travel of the rear wheels in a parallel path with the front wheels.

Tractor A motor vehicle, without a body, that has a fifth wheel and is used for pulling a semitrailer.

Tractor Protection Valve A device that automatically seals off the tractor air supply from the trailer air supply when the tractor system pressure drops to 30 or 40 psi (207 to 276 kPa).

Tractor/Trailer Lift Suspension A single axle air ride suspension with lift capabilities commonly used with steerable axles for pusher and tag applications.

Trailer A platform or container on wheels pulled by a car, truck, or tractor.

Trailer Hand Control Valve A device located on the dash or steering column and used to apply only the trailer brakes; primarily used in jackknife situations.

Trailer Slider A movable trailer suspension frame that is capable of changing trailer wheelbase by sliding and locking into different positions.

Transfer Case An additional gearbox located between the main transmission and the rear axle to transfer power from the transmission to the front and rear driving axles.

Transistor An electronic device produced by joining three sections of semiconductor materials. Like the diode, it is very useful as a switching device, functioning as either a conductor or an insulator.

Transmission A device used to transmit torque at various ratios and that can usually also change the direction of the force of rotation.

Transverse Vibrations A condition caused by an unbalanced driveline or bending movements, in the drive shaft.

Treadle A dual brake valve that releases air from the service reservoirs to the service lines and brake chambers. The valve includes a piston which pushes on diaphragms to open ports; these vent air to service lines in the primary and secondary systems.

Treadle Valve A foot-operated brake valve that controls air pressure to the service chambers.

Tree Diagnosis Chart A chart used to provide a logical sequence for what should be inspected or tested when troubleshooting a repair problem.

Triaxle Suspension A suspension consisting of three axles with a means of equalizing weight between axles.

Trunnion The end of the universal cross; they are case hardened ground surfaces on which the needle bearings ride.

TTMA An abbreviation for Truck and Trailer Manufacturers Association.

Turbine The output (driven) member that is splined to the forward clutch of the transmission and to the turbine shaft assembly.

TVW An abbreviation for (1) Total vehicle weight. (2) Towed vehicle weight.

Two-Speed Axle Assembly An axle assembly having two different output ratios from the differential. The driver selects the ratios from the controls located in the cab of the truck.

U-Bolt A fastener used to clamp the top U-bolt plate, spring, axle, and bottom U-bolt plate together. Inverted (nuts down) U-bolts cross springs when in place; conventional (nuts up) U-bolts wrap around the axle.

UNEP An abbreviation for United Nations Environment Program. Mandates the complete phaseout of CFC-based refrigerants by 1995.

Underslung Suspension A suspension in which the spring is positioned under the axle.

United Nations Environmental Program (UNEP) A protocol that mandated the complete phase-out of CFC-based refrigerants by the year 1995.

Universal Gladhand A term often used for non-polarized gladhand.

Universal Joint (U-joint) A component that allows torque to be transmitted to components that are operating at different angles.

Upper Coupler The flat load-bearing surface under the front of a semitrailer, including the kingpin, which rests firmly on the fifth wheel when coupled.

Vacuum Air below atmospheric pressure. There are three types of vacuums important to engine and component function: manifold vacuum, ported vacuum, and venturi vacuum. The strength of either of these vacuums depend on throttle opening, engine speed, and load.

Validity List A list supplied by the manufacturer of valid bulletins.

Valve Body and Governor Test Stand A specialized piece of test equipment. The valve body of the transmission is removed from the vehicle and mounted into the test stand. The test stand duplicates all vehicle running conditions, so the valve body can be thoroughly tested and calibrated.

Variable Pitch Stator A stator design often used in torque converters in off-highway applications such as dirt and stone aggregate dump or haul trucks, or other specialized equipment used to transport unusually heavy loads in rough terrain.

Vehicle Body Clearance (VBC) The distance from the inside of the inner tire to the spring or other body structures.

Vehicle On-board Radar (VORAD) A system similar to an electronic eye that constantly monitors other vehicles on the road to give the driver additional reaction time to respond to potential dangers.

Vehicle Retarder An optional type of braking device that has been developed and successfully used over the years to supplement or assist the service brakes on heavy-duty trucks.

Vertical Load Capacity The maximum, recommended vertical downward force that can be safely applied to a coupling device.

VIN An abbreviation for Vehicle Identification Number.

Viscosity The ability of an oil to maintain proper lubricating quality under various conditions of operating speed, temperature, and pressure. Viscosity describes oil thickness or resistance to flow.

Volt The unit of electromotive force.

Voltage Generating Sensors These are devices which produces their own input voltage signal.

Voltage Limiter A device that provides protection by limiting voltage to the instrument panel gauges to approximately 5 volts.

Voltage Regulator A device that controls the amount of current produced by the alternator or generator and thus the voltage level in the charging circuit.

VORAD An acronym for Vehicle On-board Radar.

Vortex Oil Flow The circular flow that occurs as the oil is forced from the impeller to the turbine and then back to the impeller.

Watt The measure of electrical power.

Watt's Law A basic law of electricity used to find the power of an electrical circuit expressed in watts. It states that power equals the voltage multiplied by the current, in amperes.

Wear Compensator A device mounted in the clutch cover having an actuator arm that fits into a hole in the release sleeve retainer.

Wedge-Actuated Brakes A brake system using air pressure and air brake chambers to push a wedge and roller assembly into an actuator that is located between adjusting and anchor pistons.

Wet Tank A supply reservoir.

Wheel Alignment The mechanics of keeping all the parts of the steering system in the specified relation to each other.

Wheel and Axle Speed Sensors Electromagnetic devices used to monitor vehicle speed information for an antilock controller.

Wheel Balance The equal distribution of weight in a wheel with the tire mounted. It is an important factor which affects tire wear and vehicle control.

Windings (1) The three separate bundles in which wires are grouped in the stator. (2) The coil of wire found in a relay or other similar device. (3) That part of an electrical clutch that provides a magnetic field.

Work (1) Forcing a current through a resistance. (2) The product of a force.

Yield Strength The highest stress a material can stand without permanent deformation or damage, expressed in pounds per square inch (psi).

Yoke Sleeve Kit This can be installed instead of completely replacing the yoke. The sleeve is of heavy walled construction with a hardened steel surface having an outside diameter that is the same as the original yoke diameter.

Zener Diode A variation of the diode, this device functions like a standard diode until a certain voltage is reached. When the voltage level reaches this point, the zener diode will allow current to flow in the reverse direction. Zener diodes are often used in electronic voltage regulators.